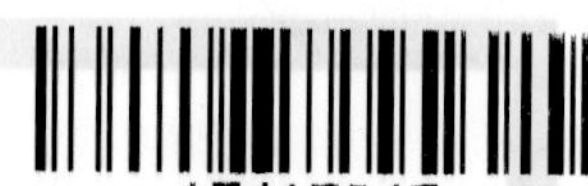
AF415047

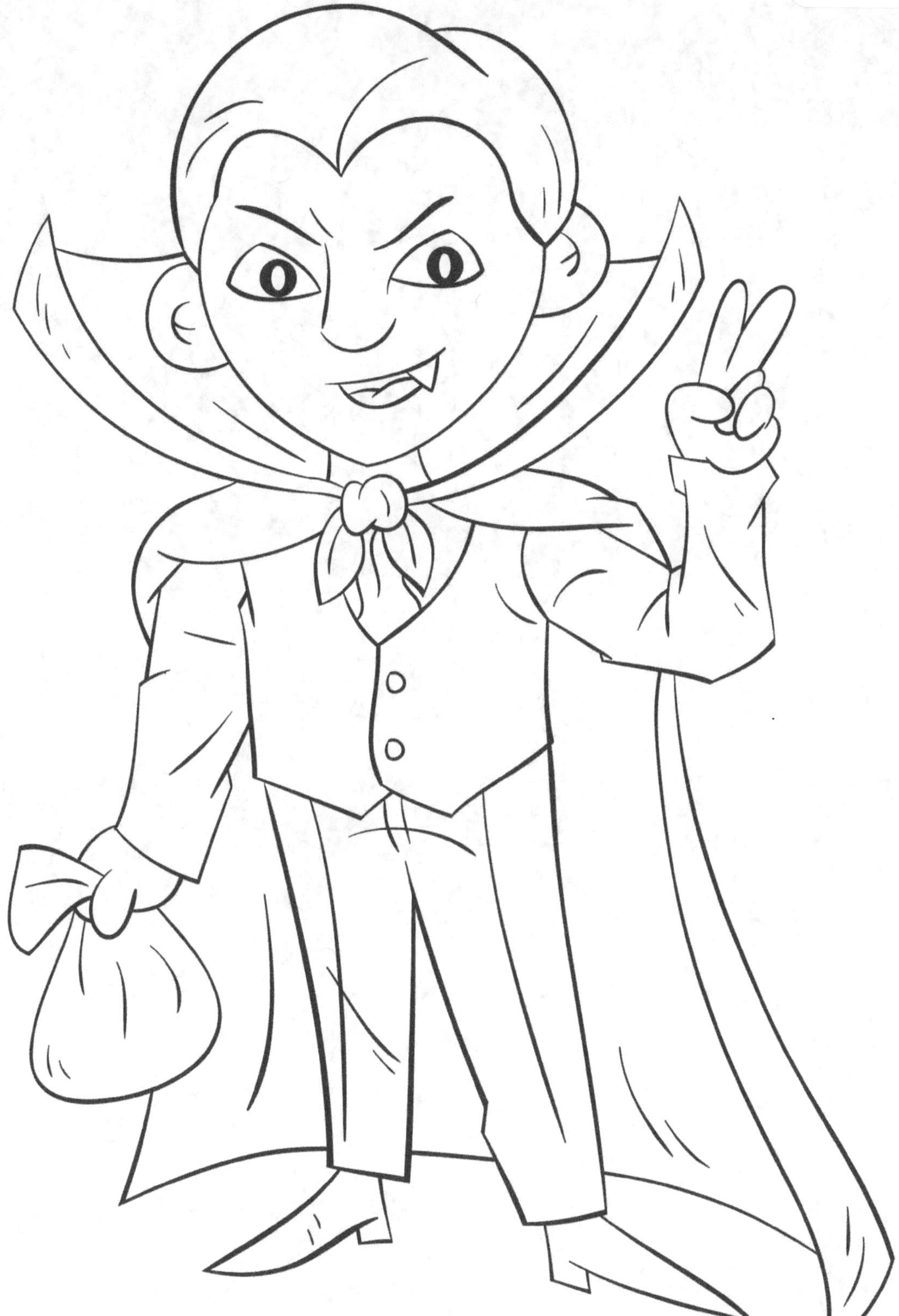

COLORARE HALLOWEEN

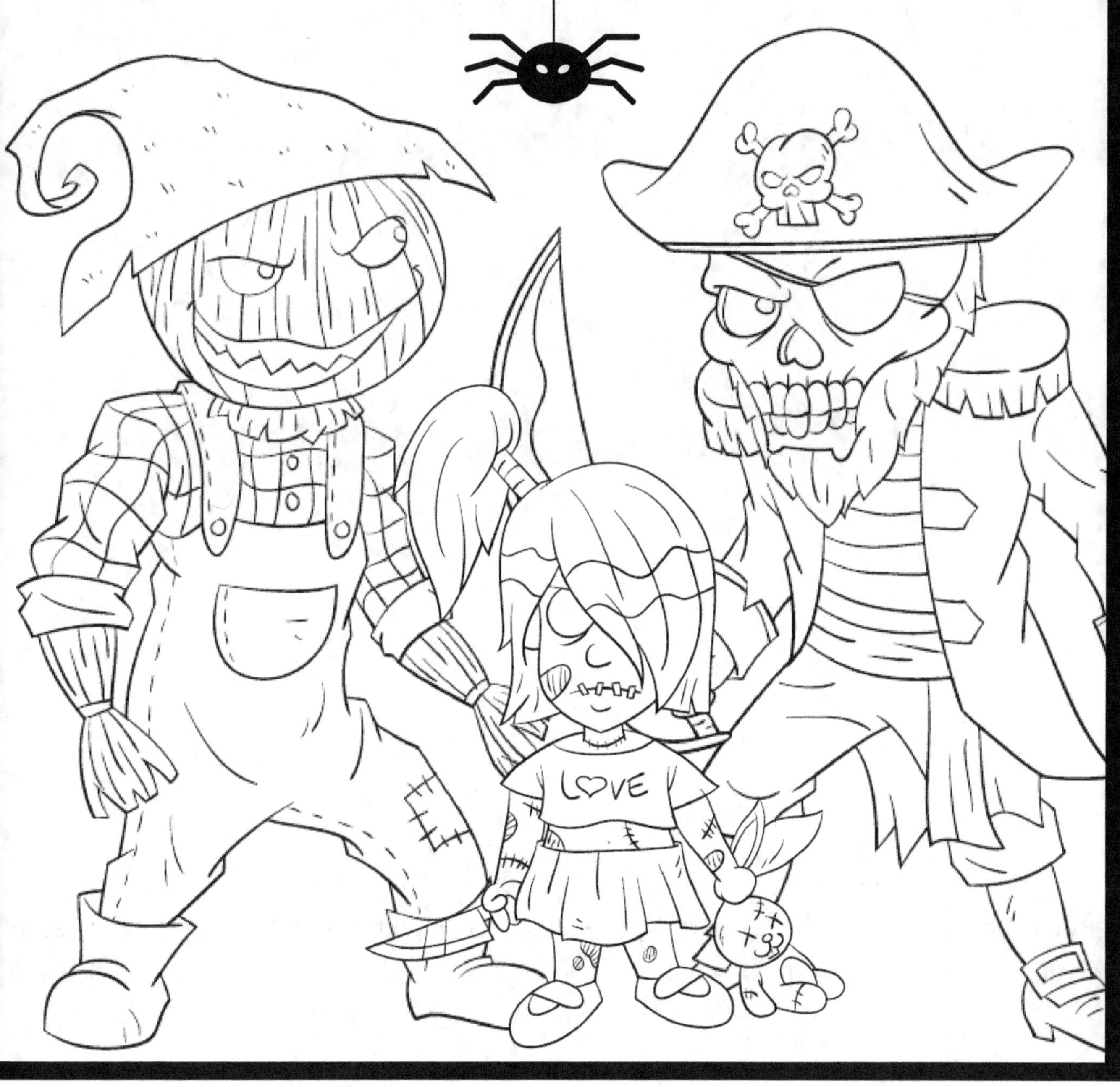

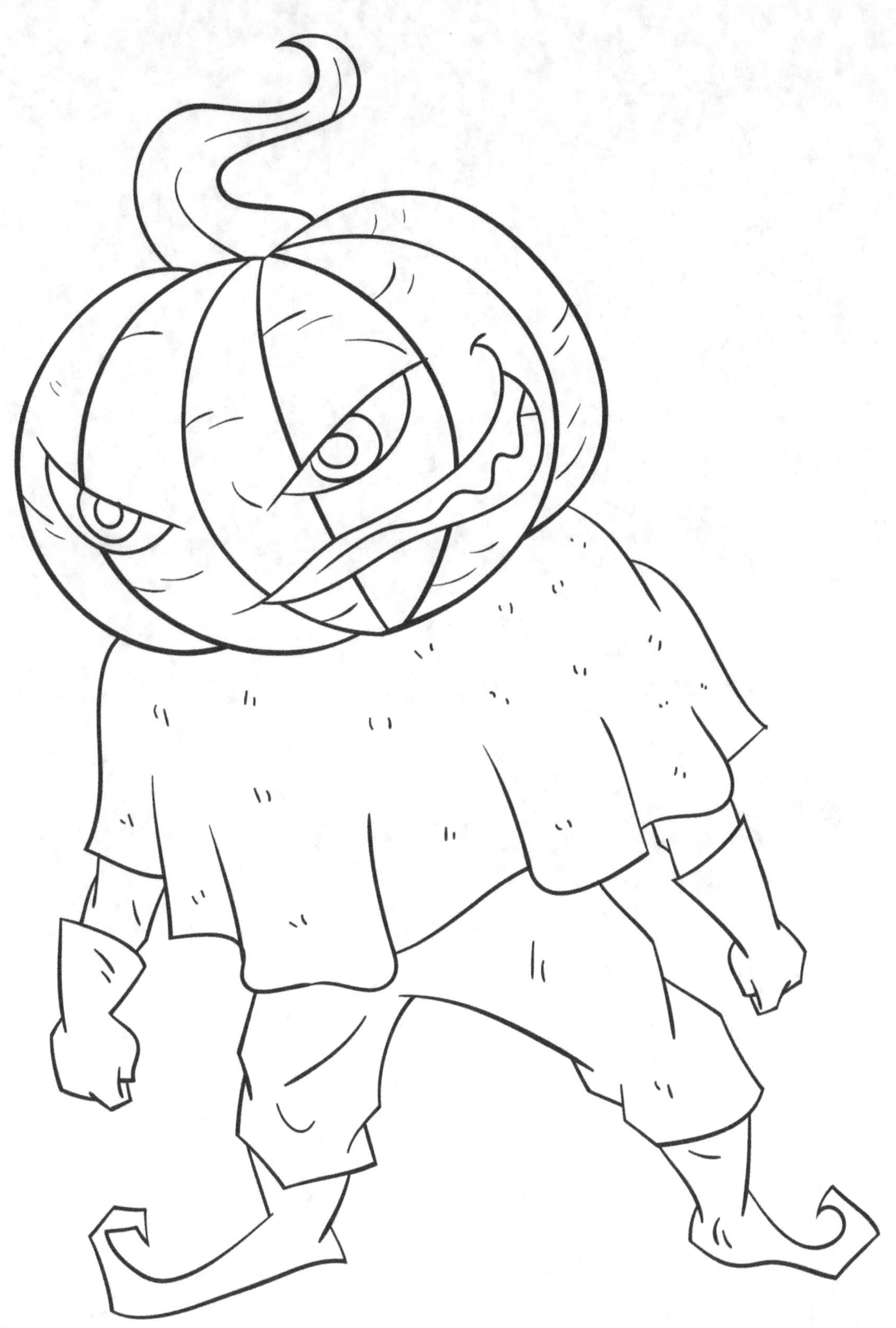

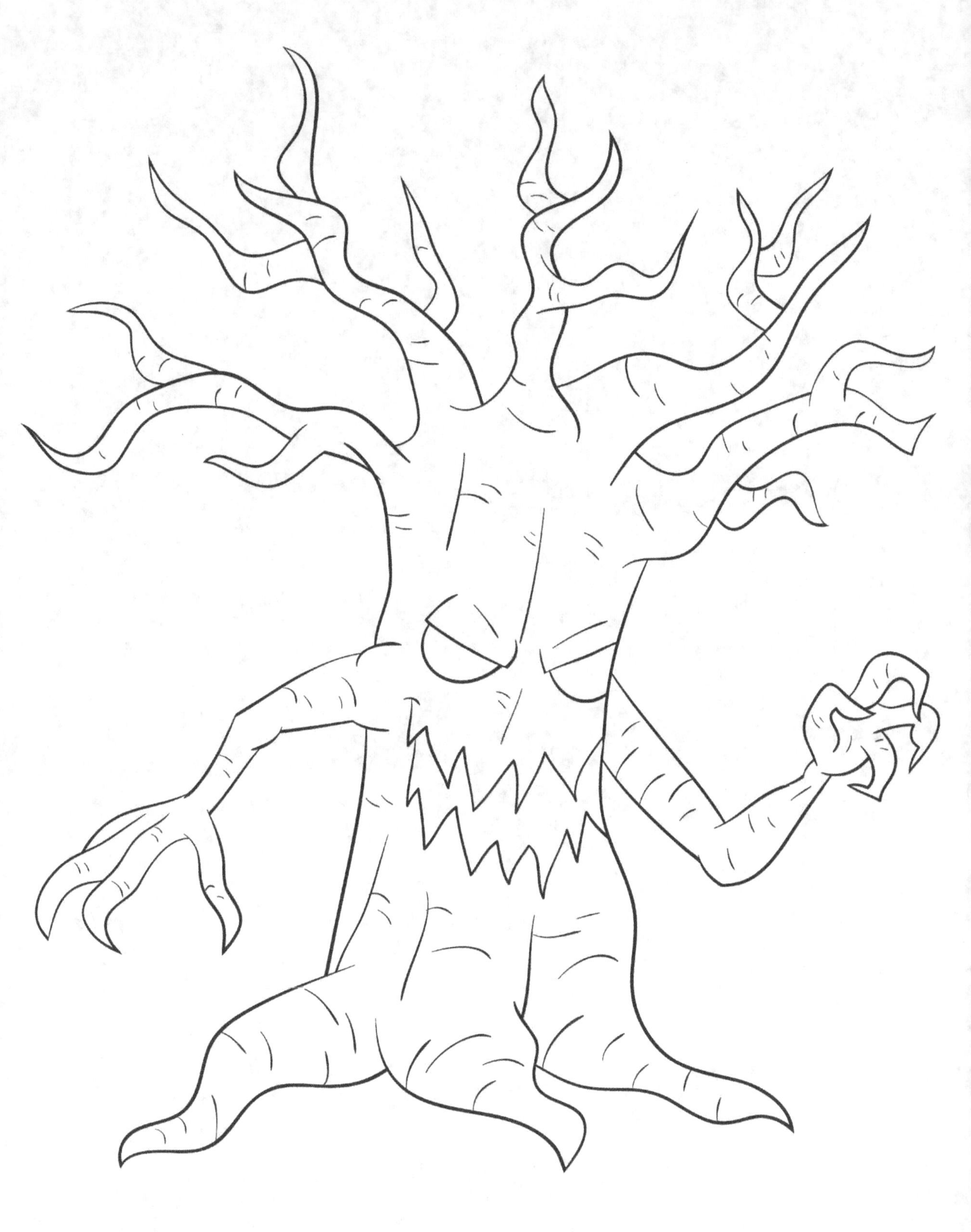

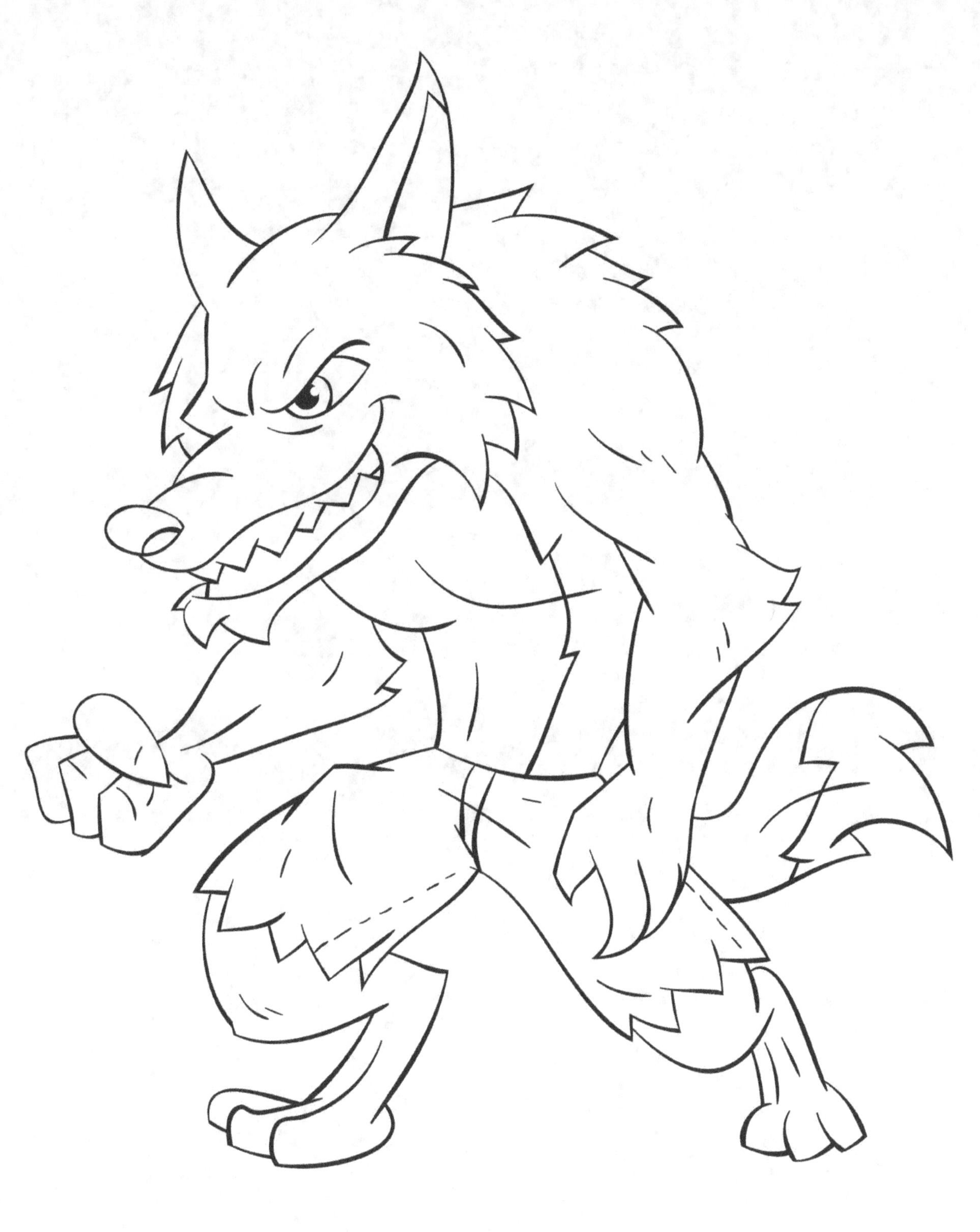

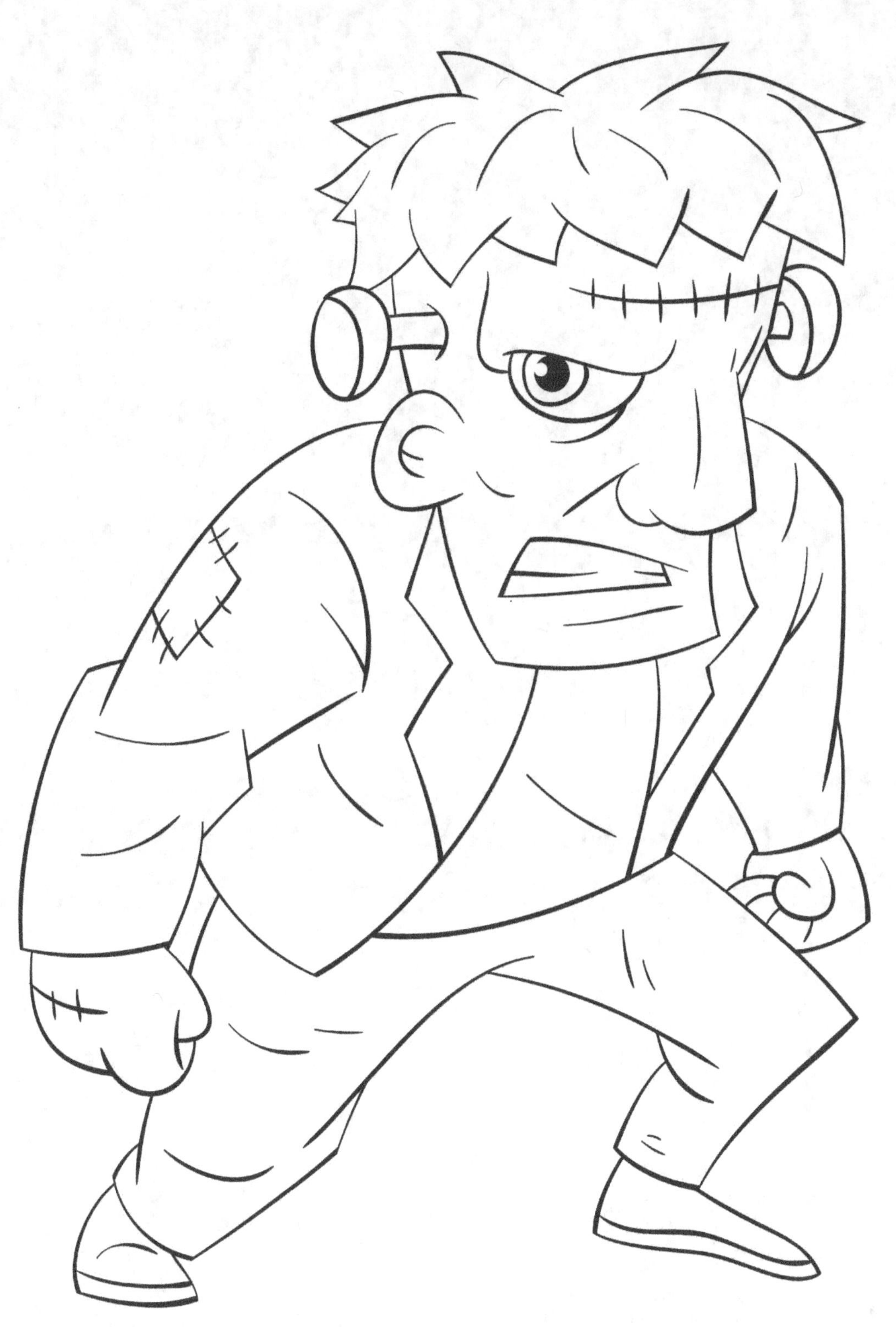

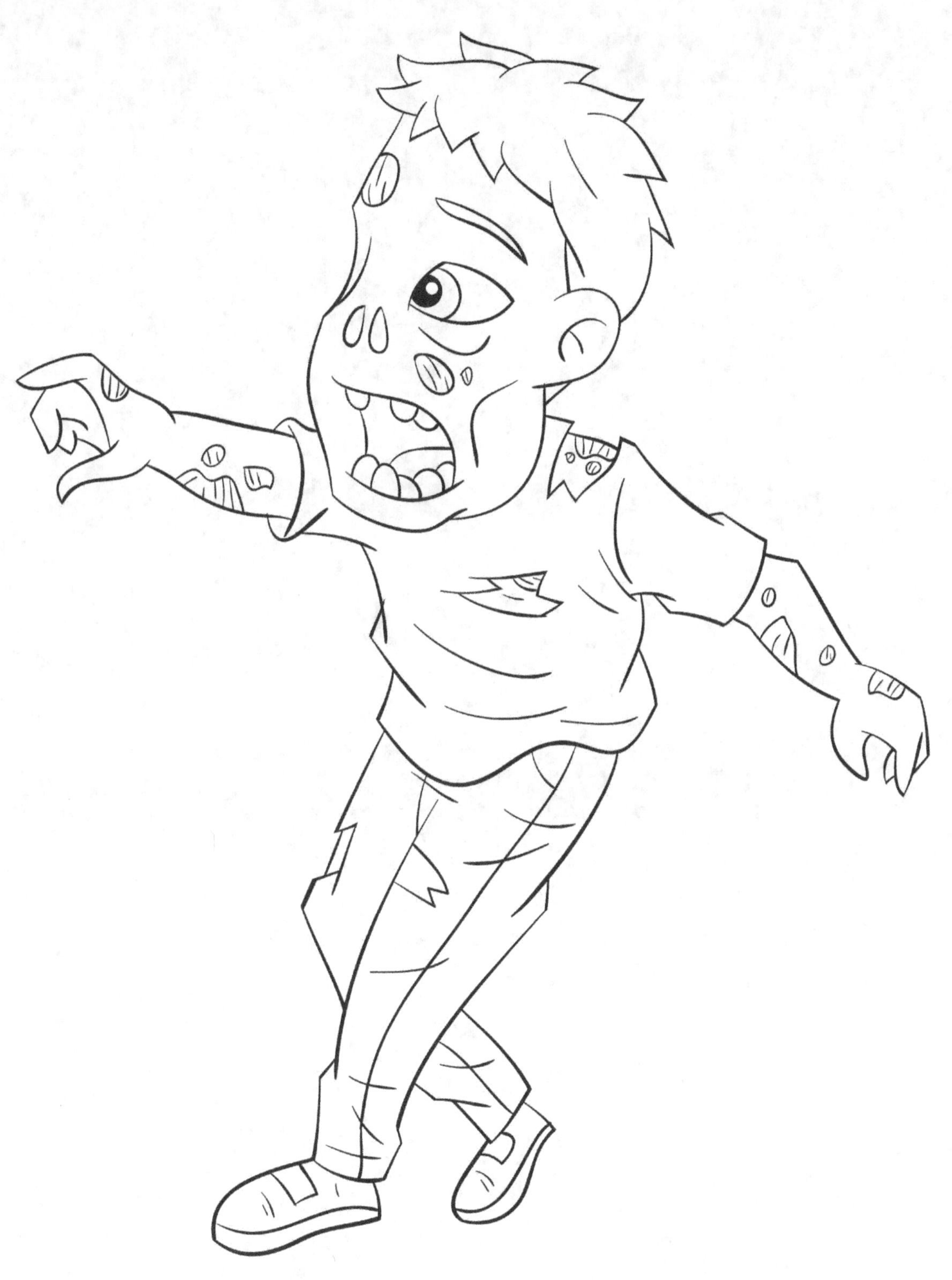

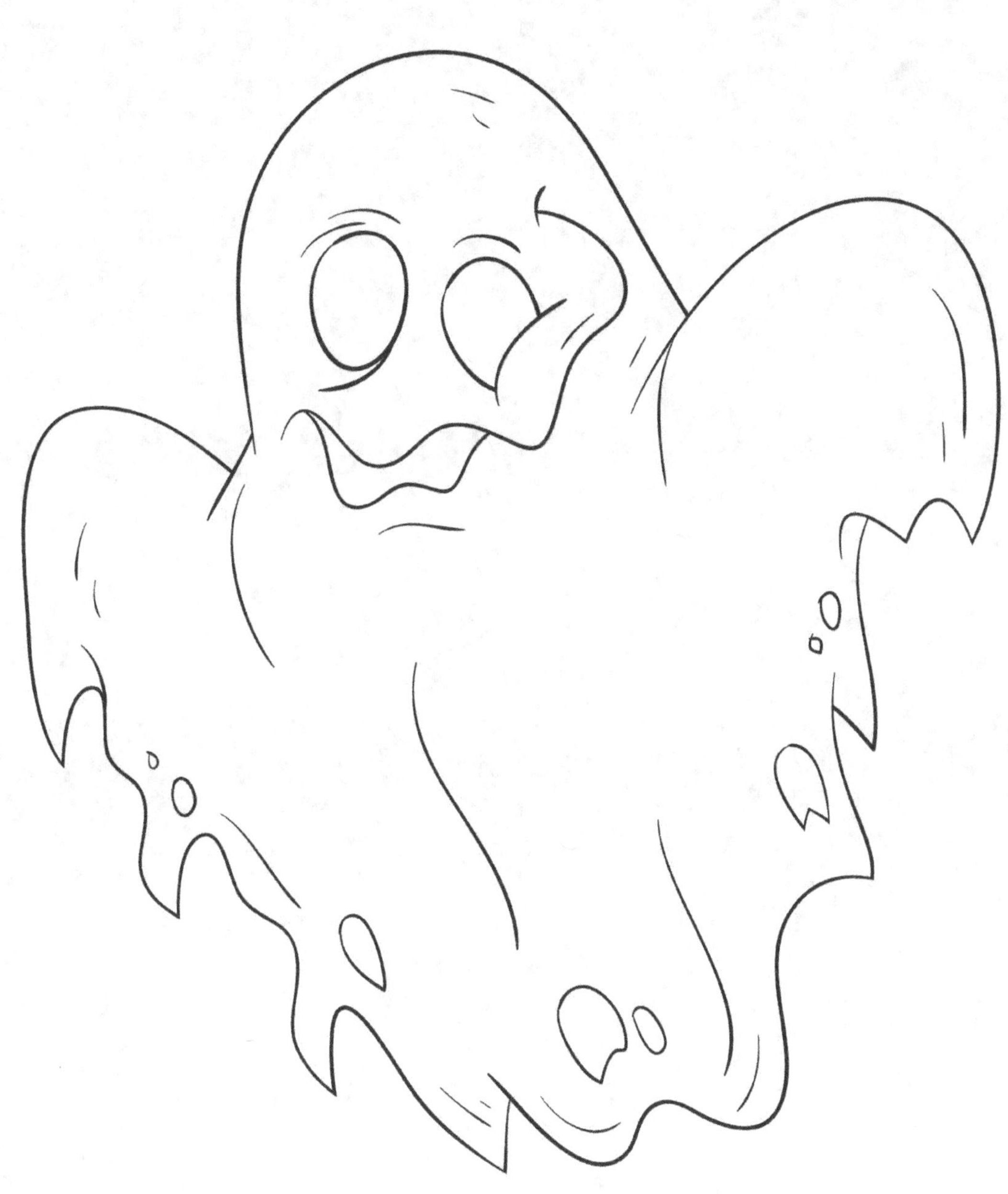

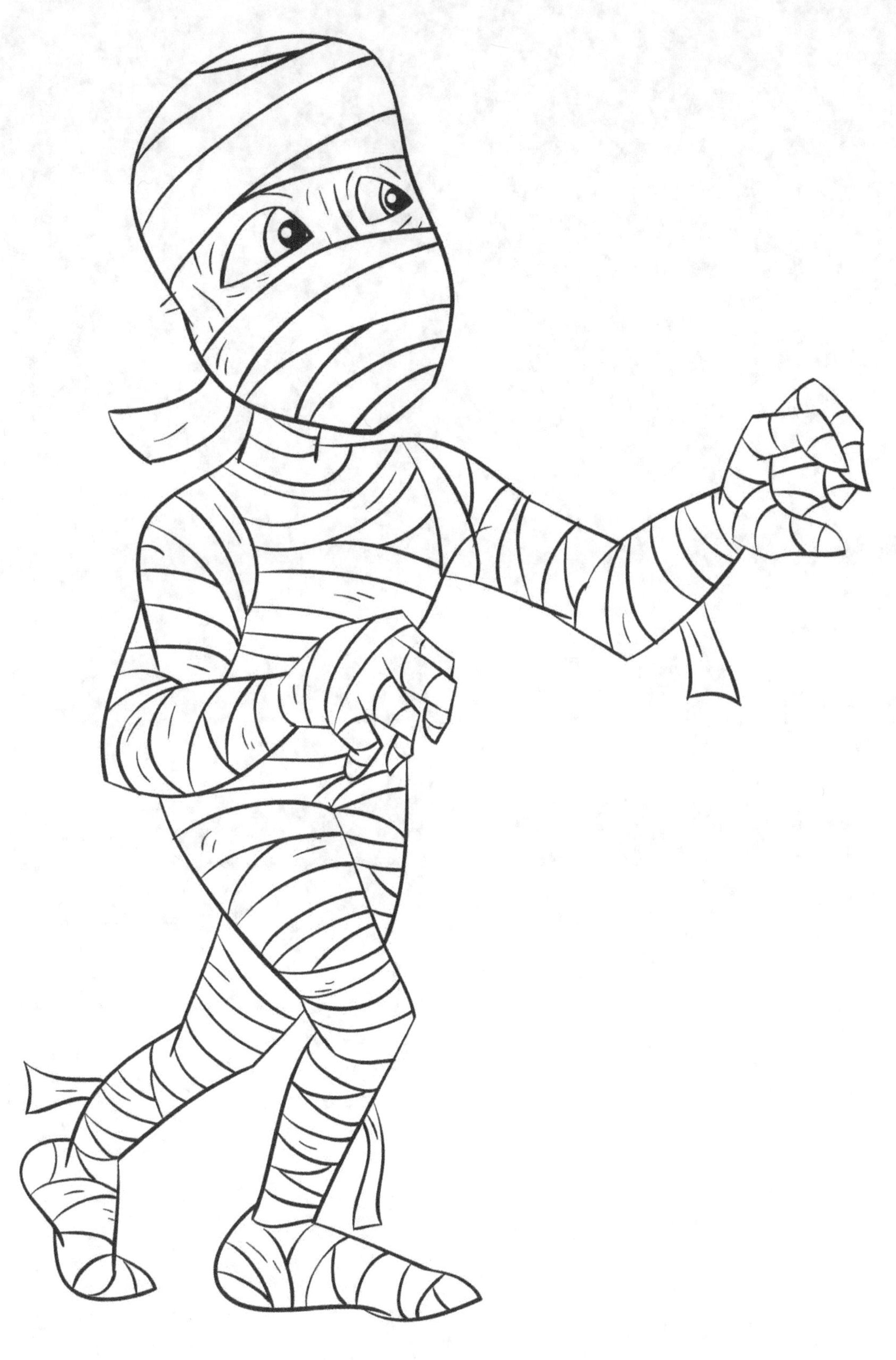

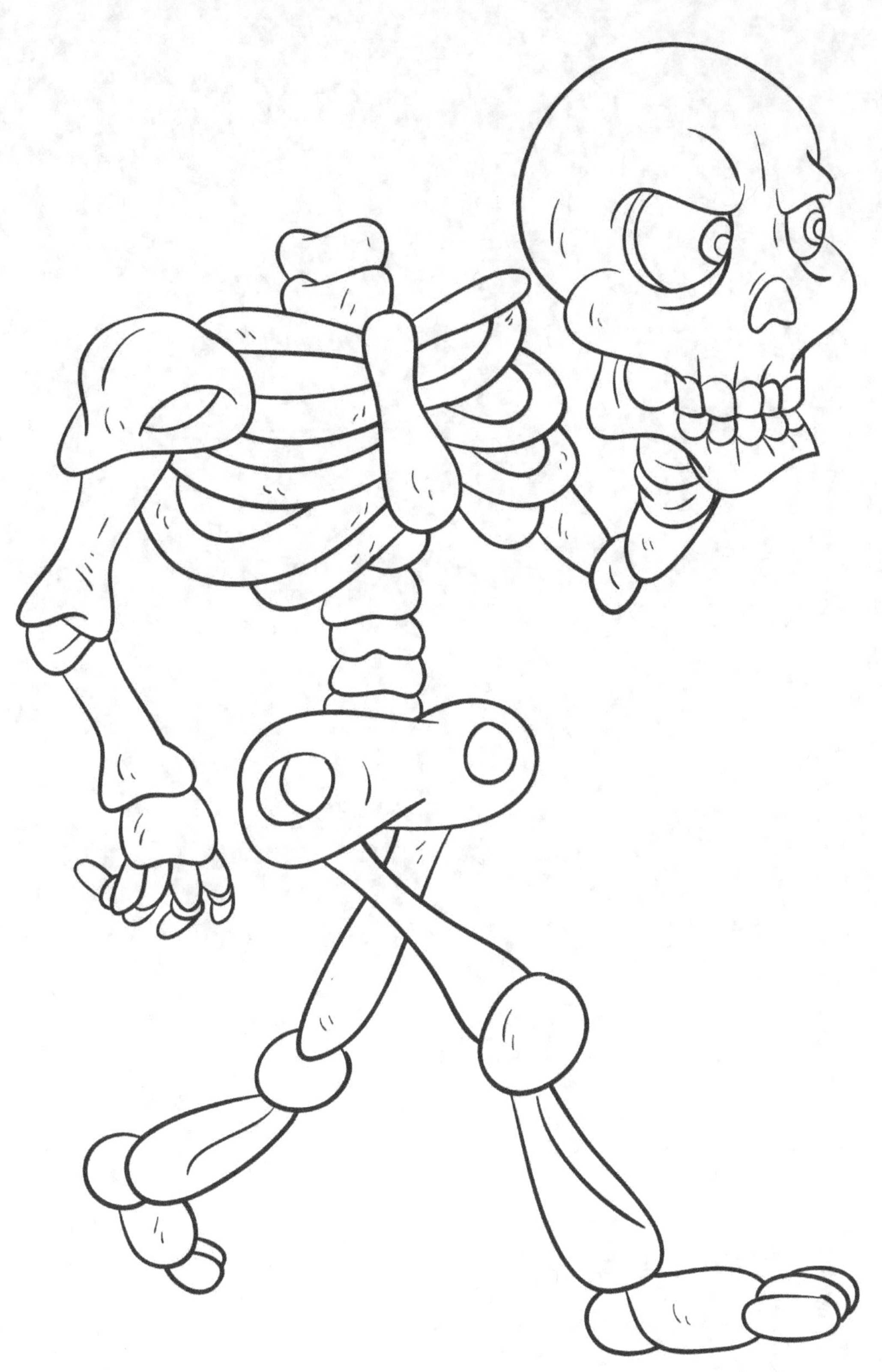

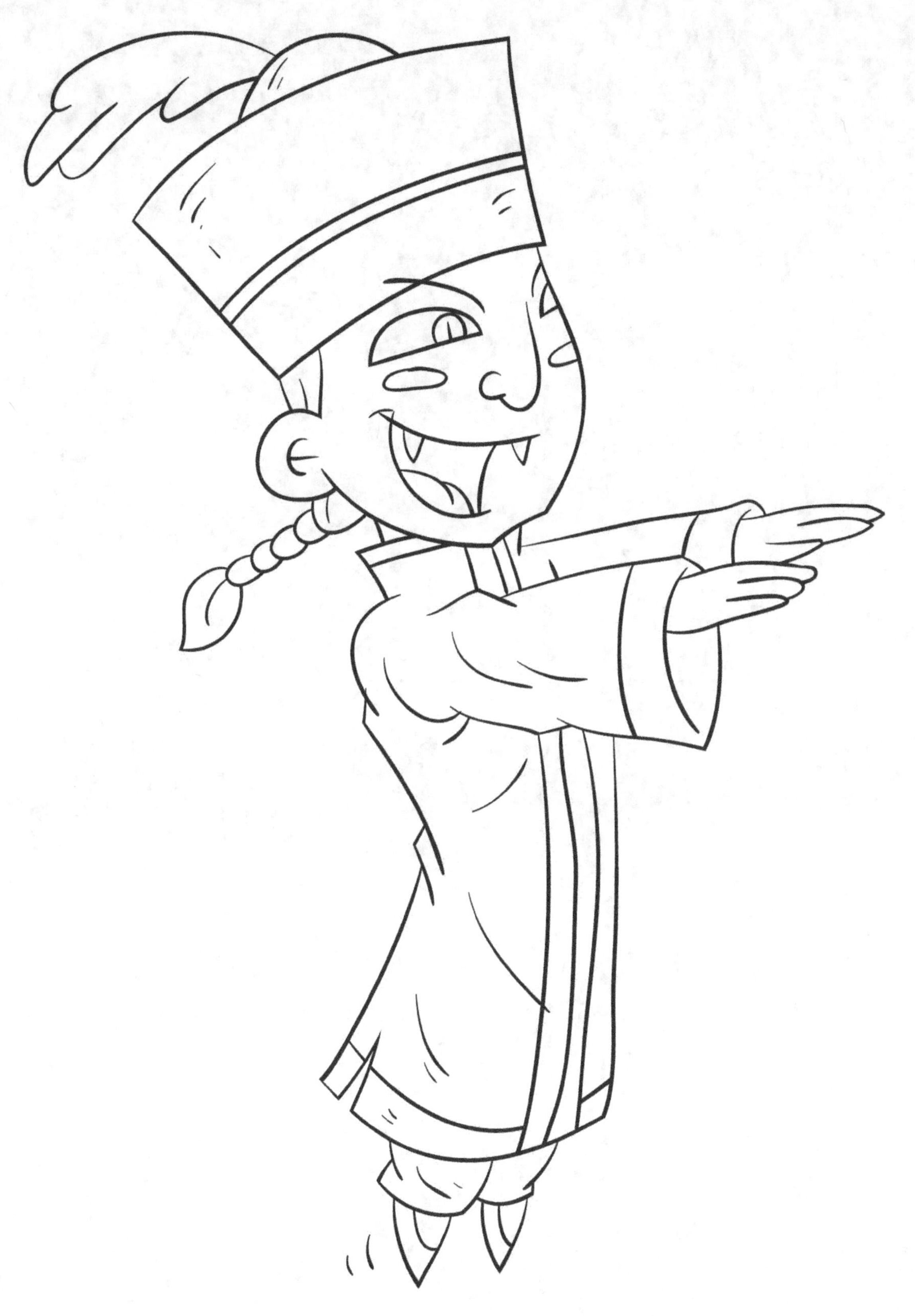

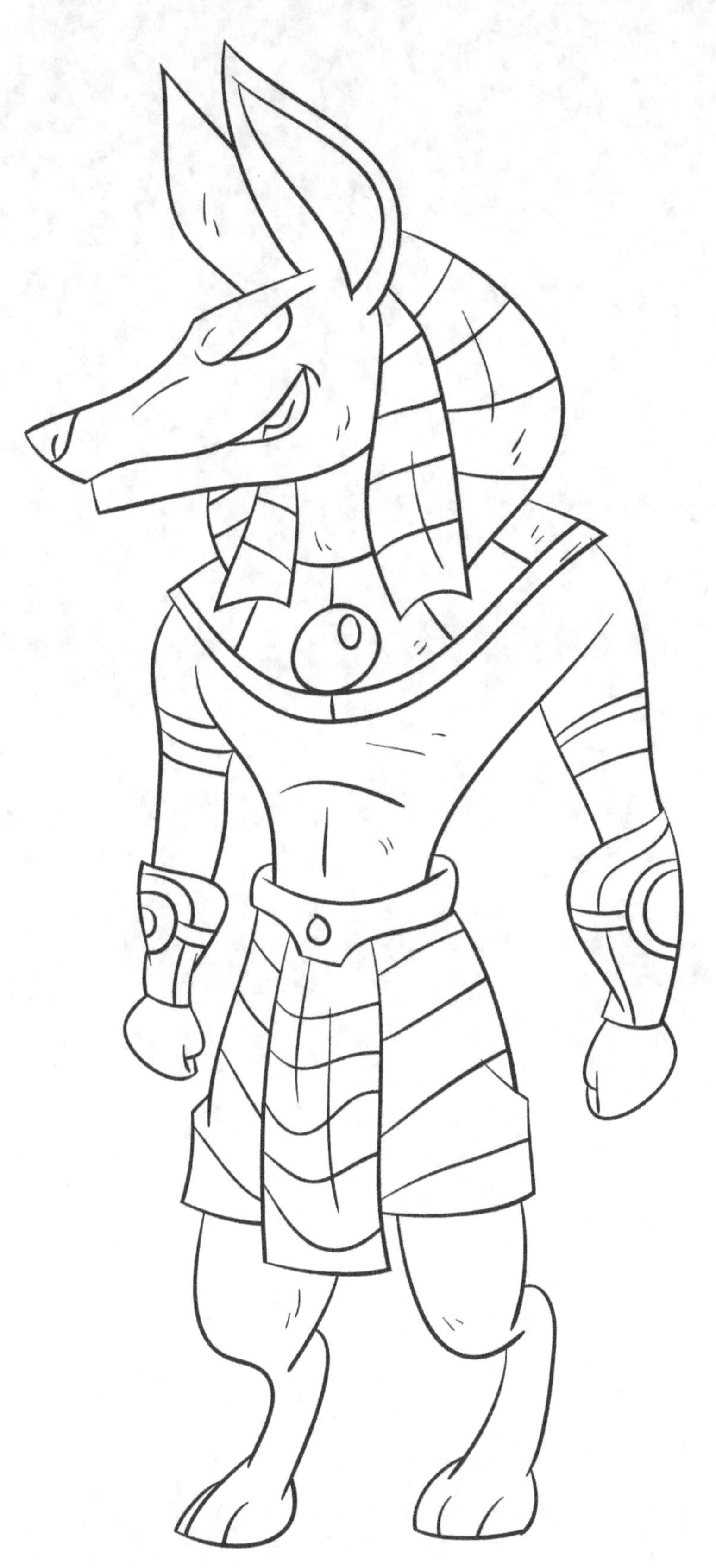

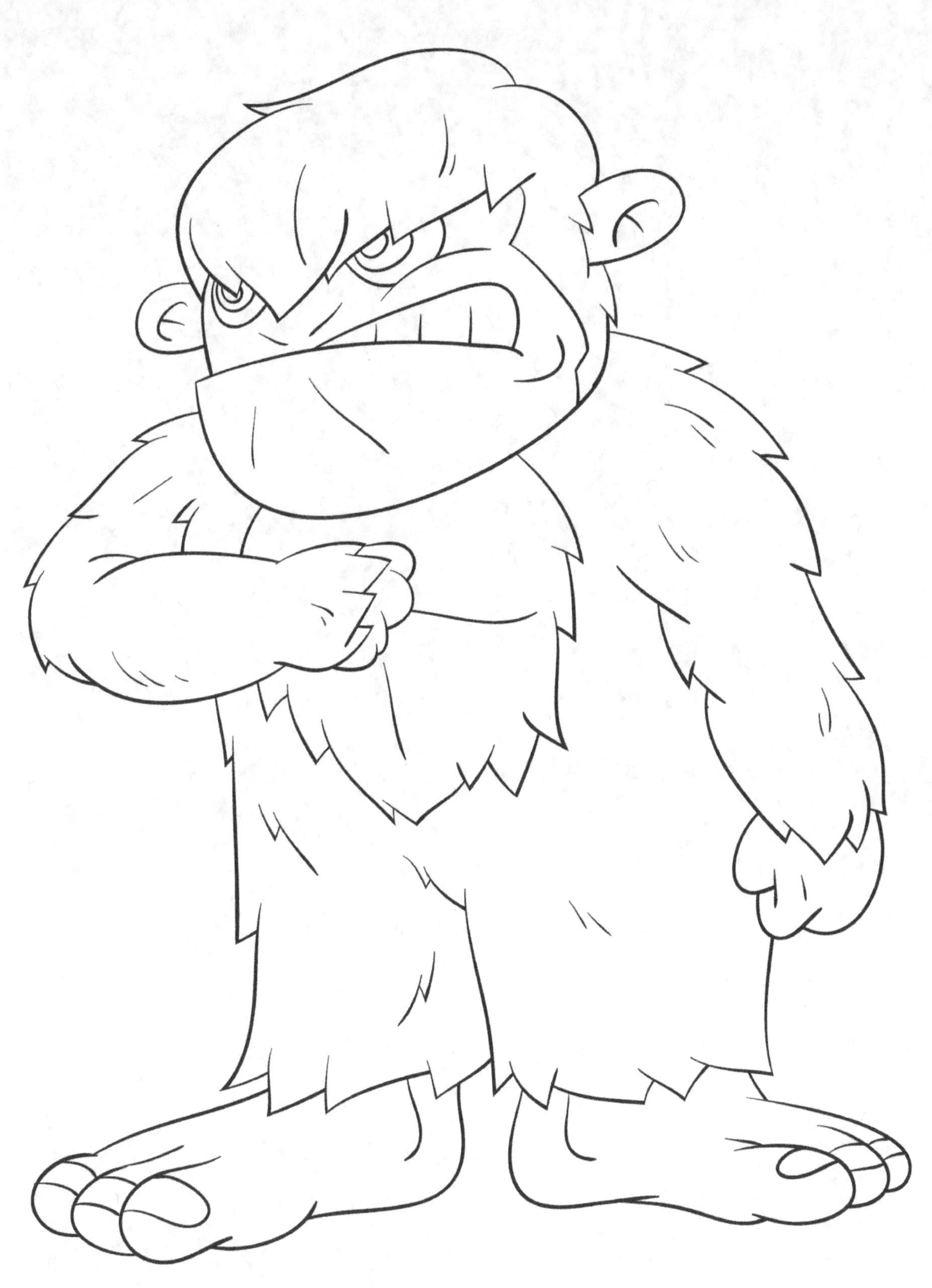

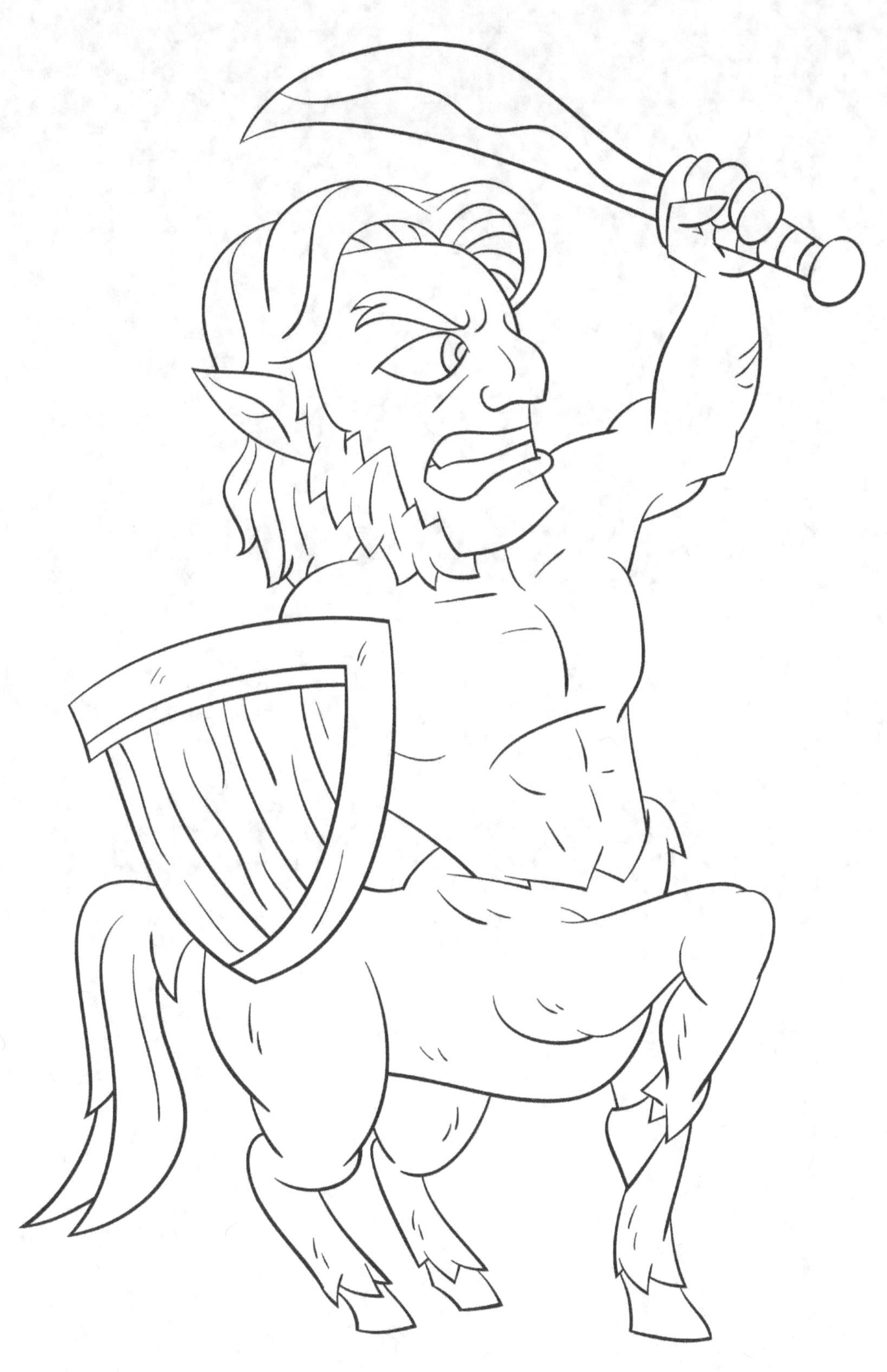

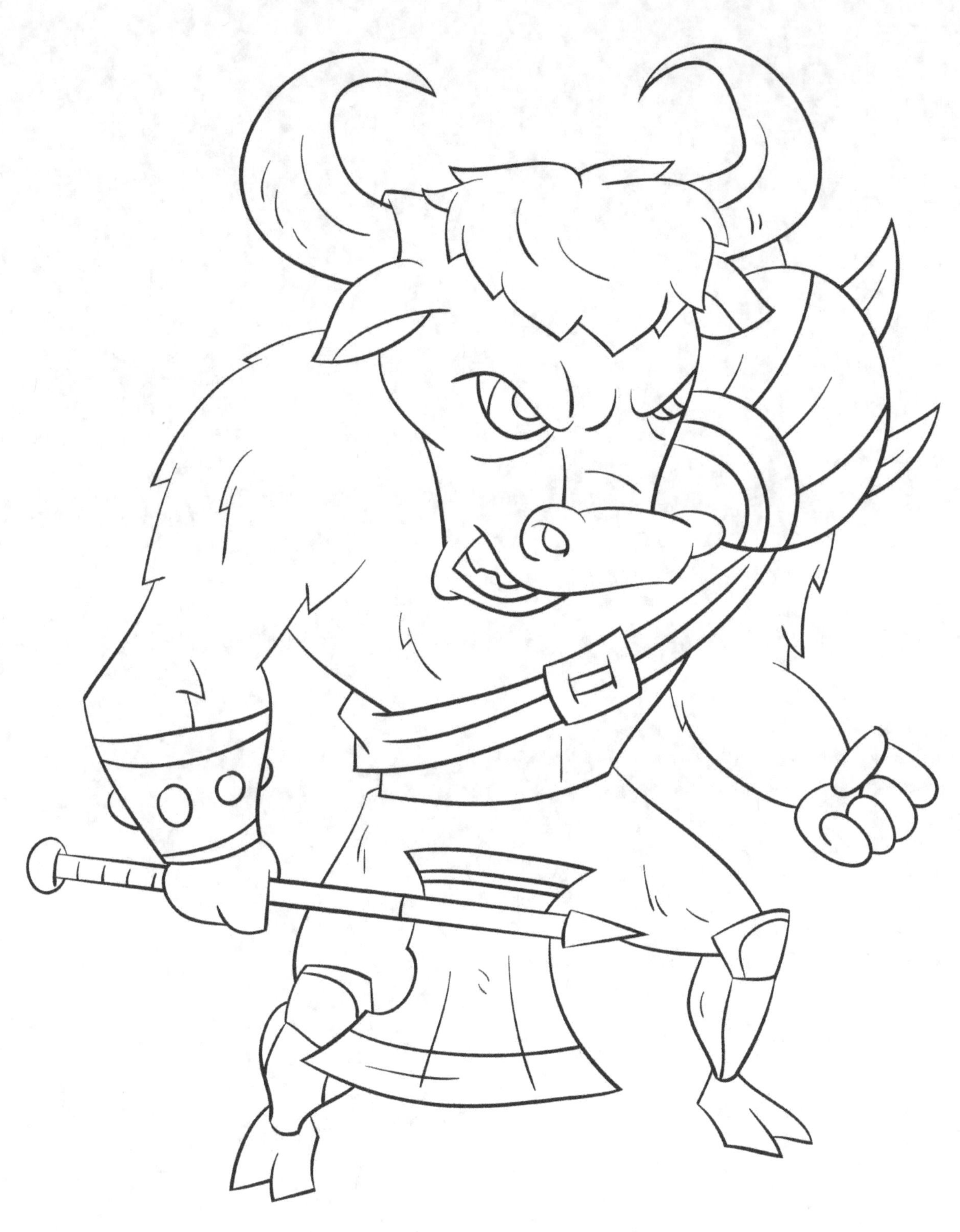

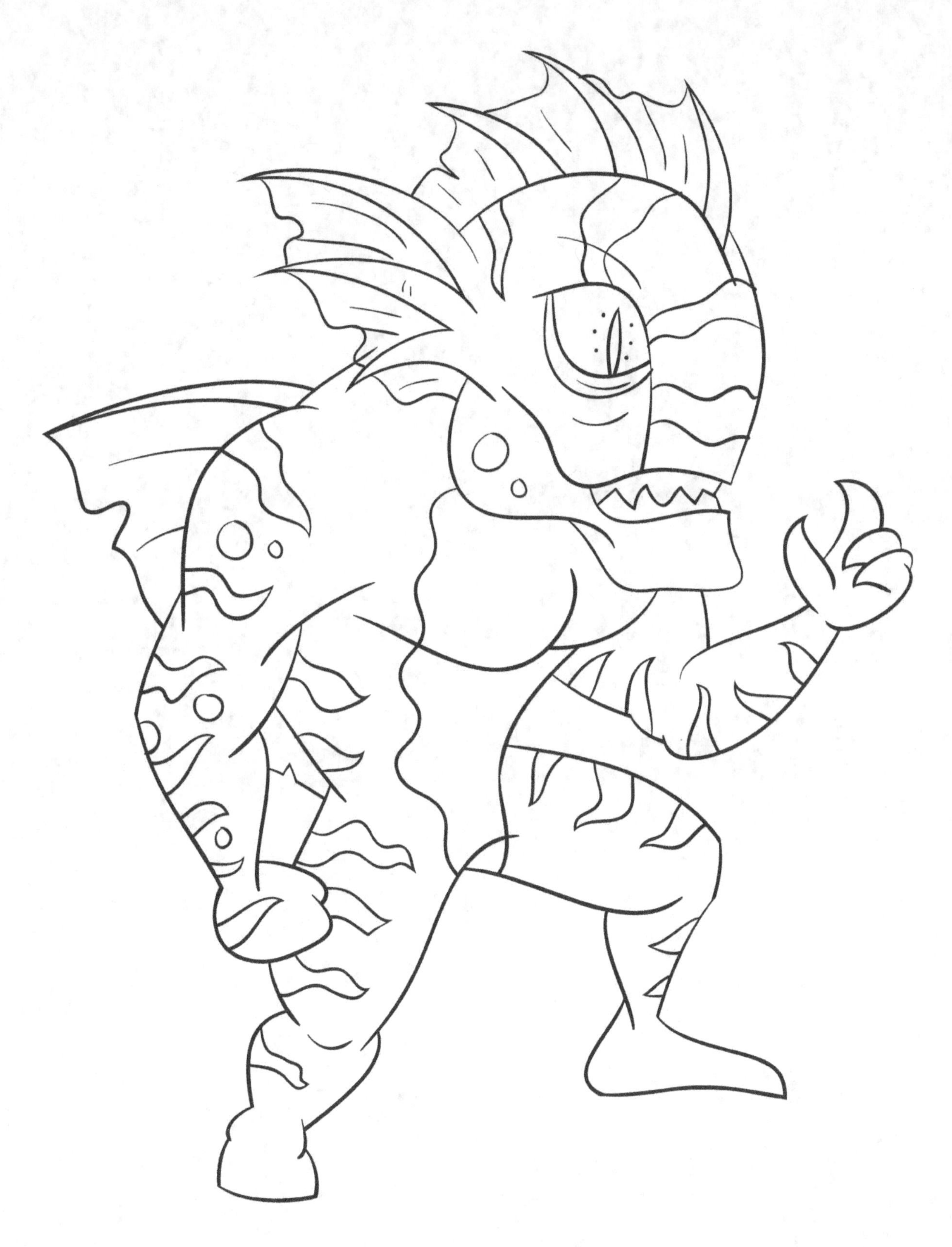

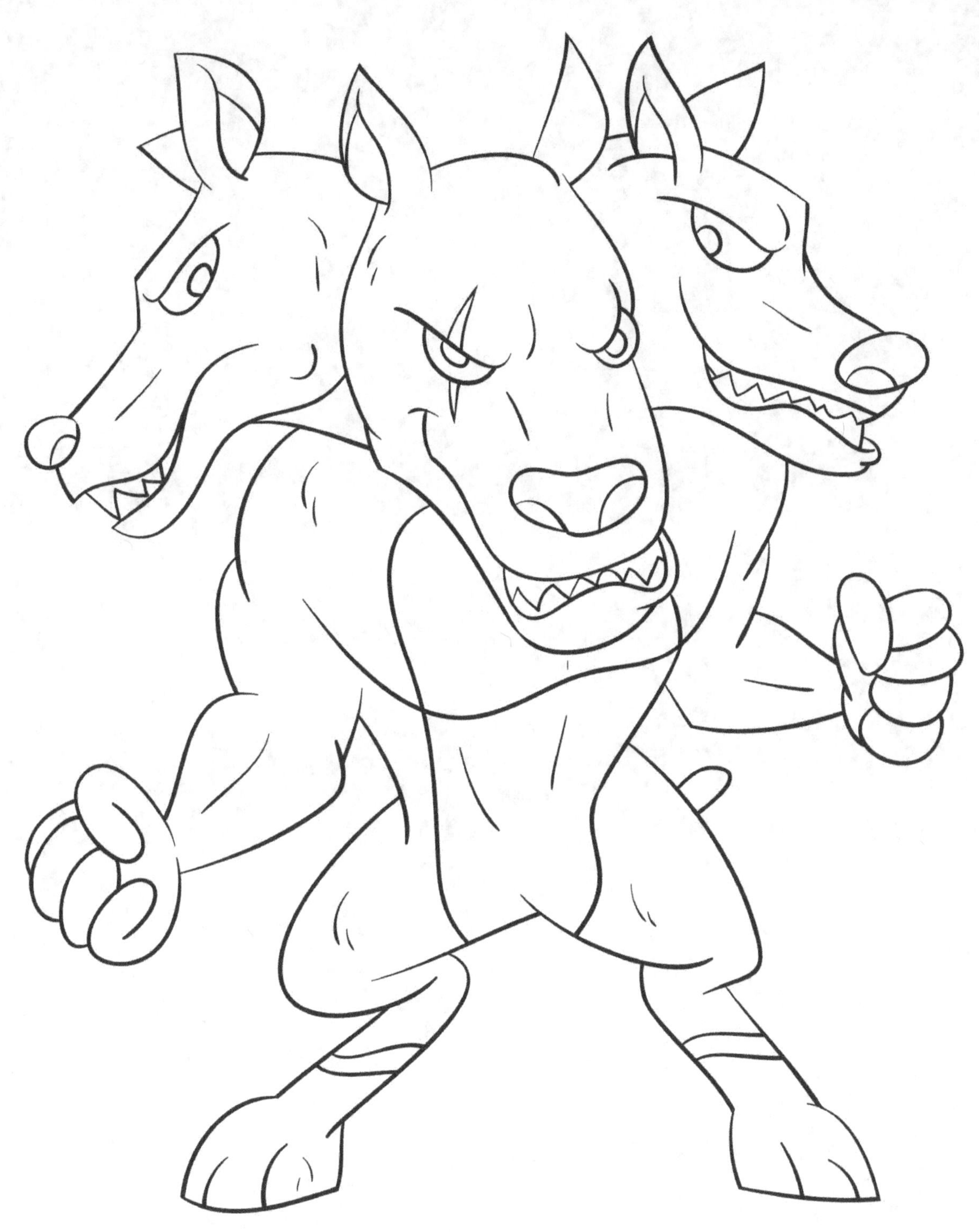

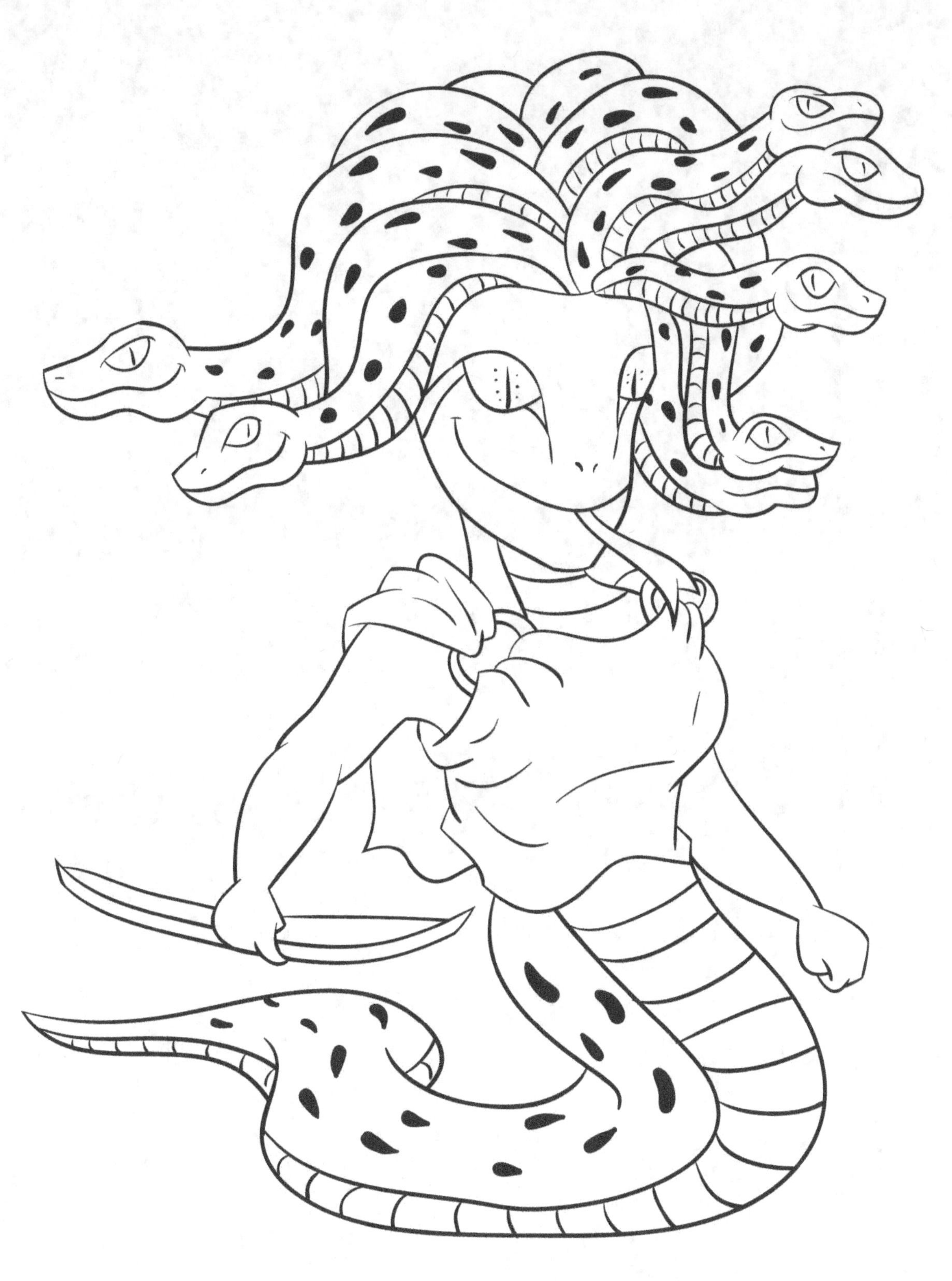

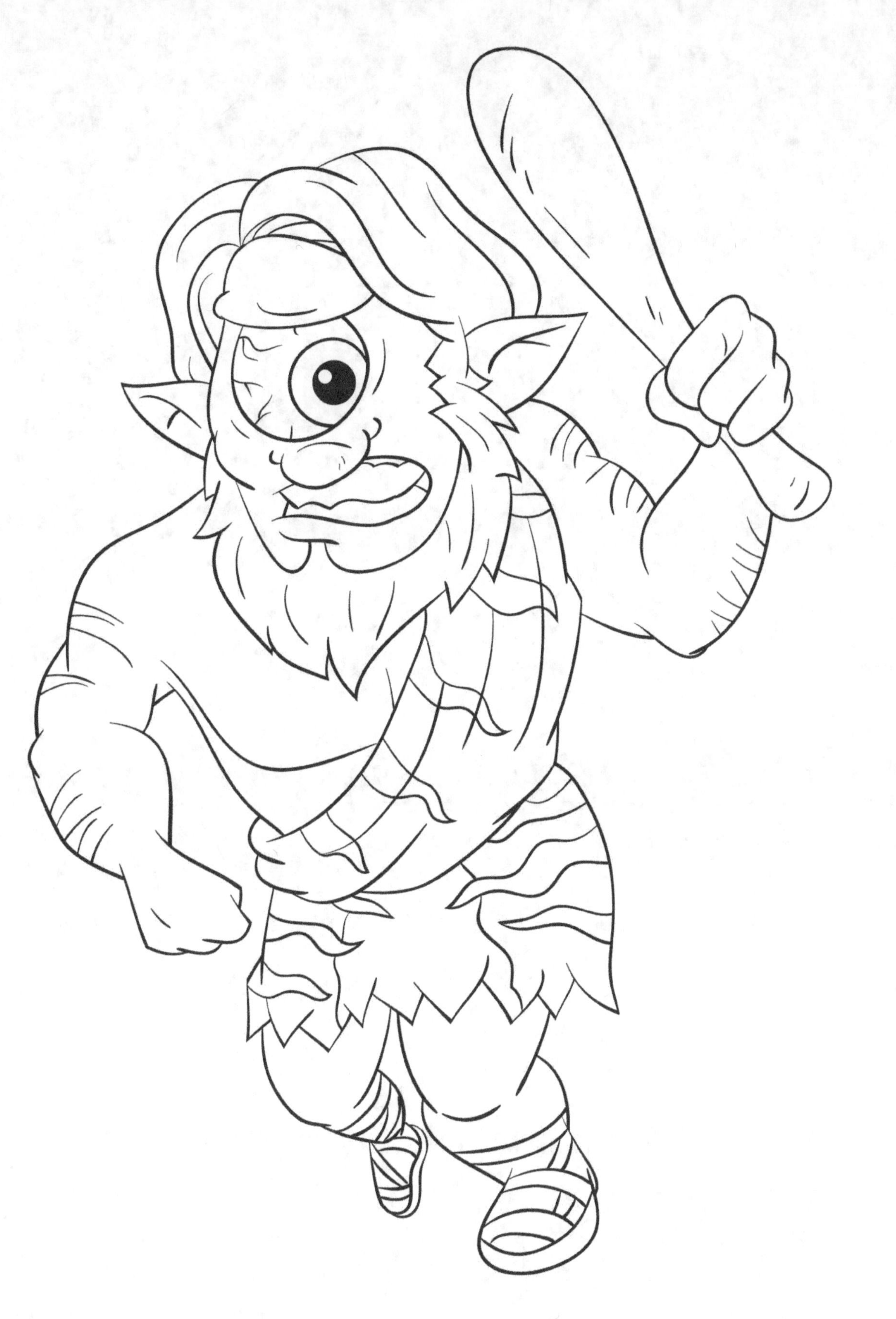

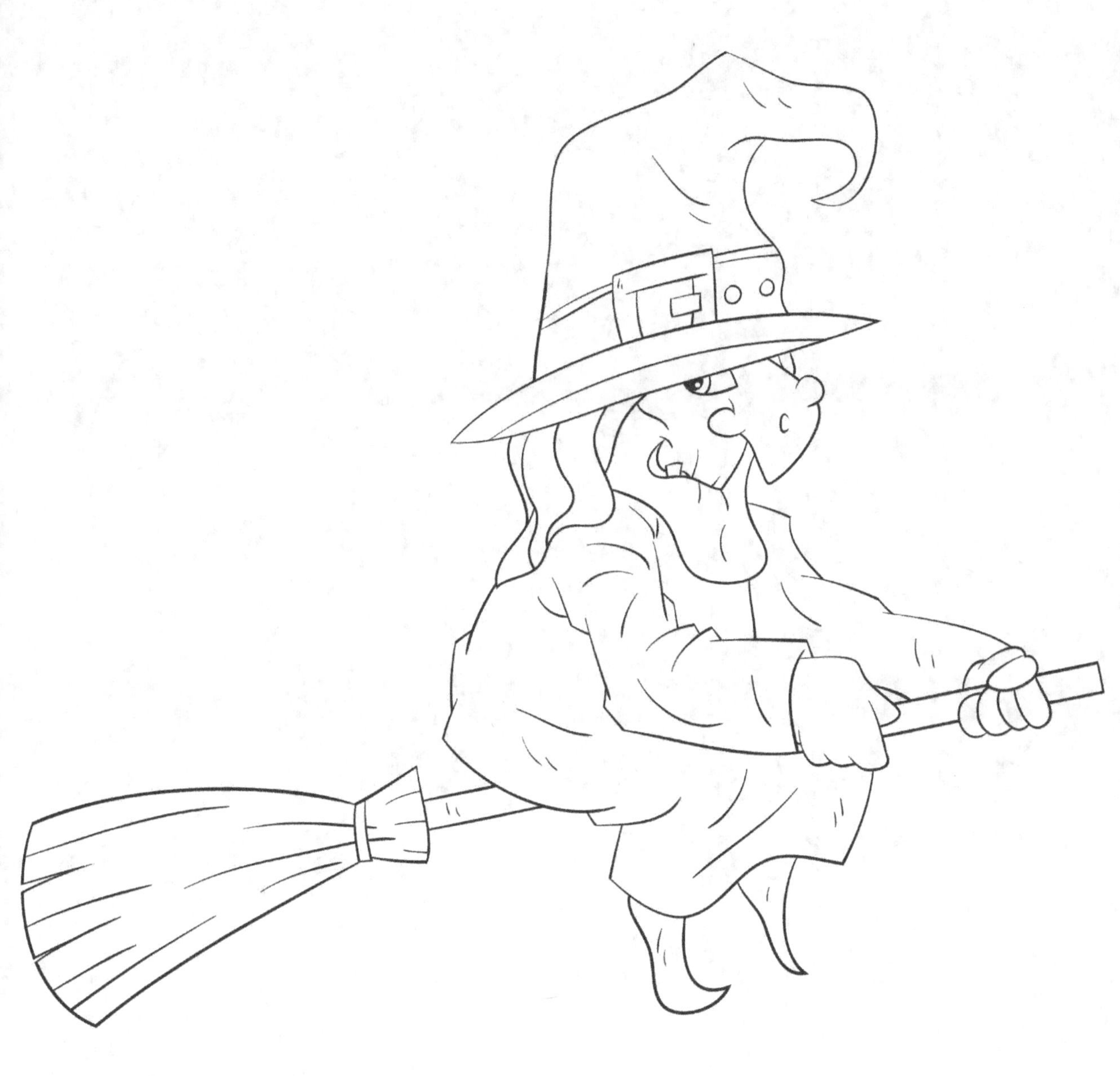

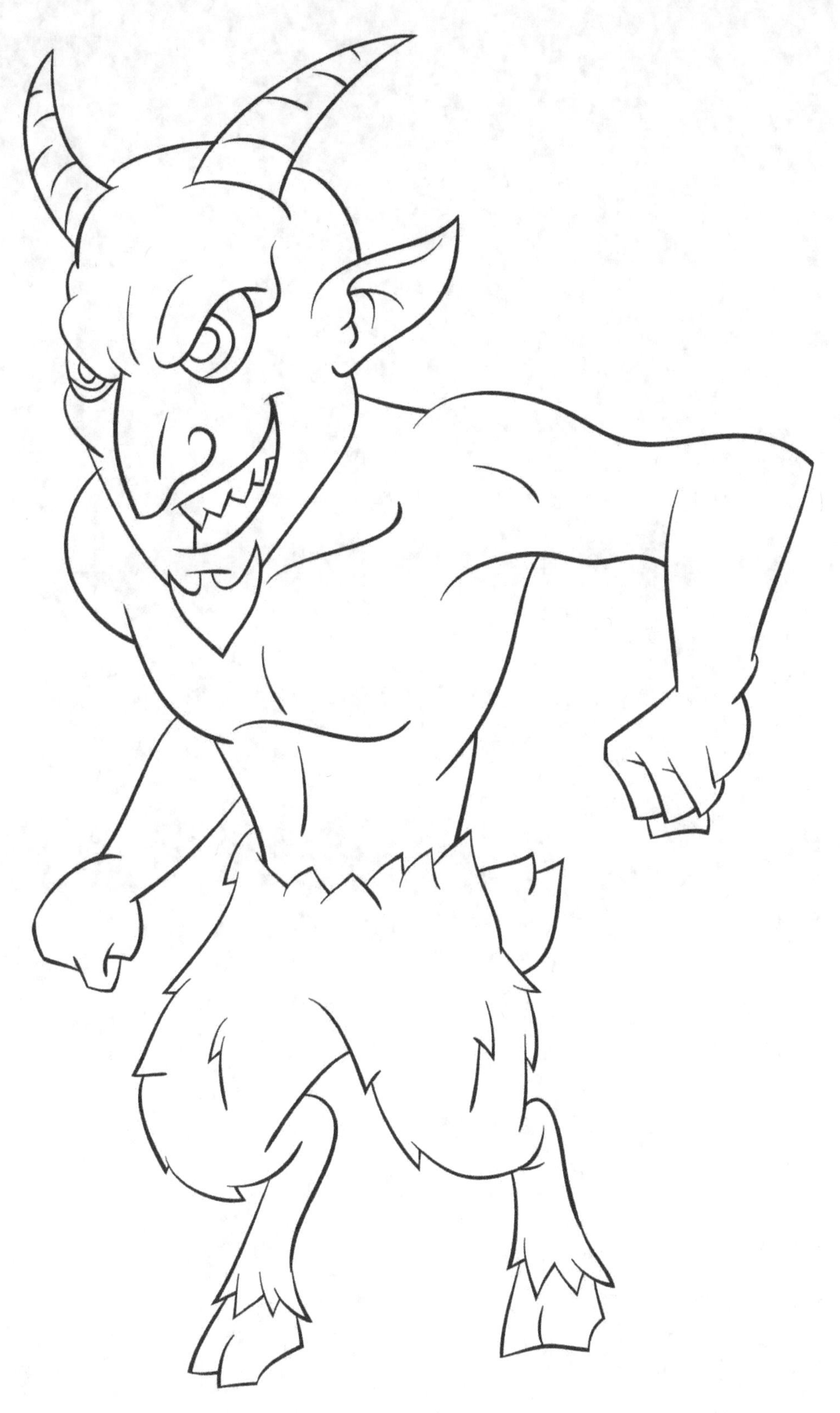

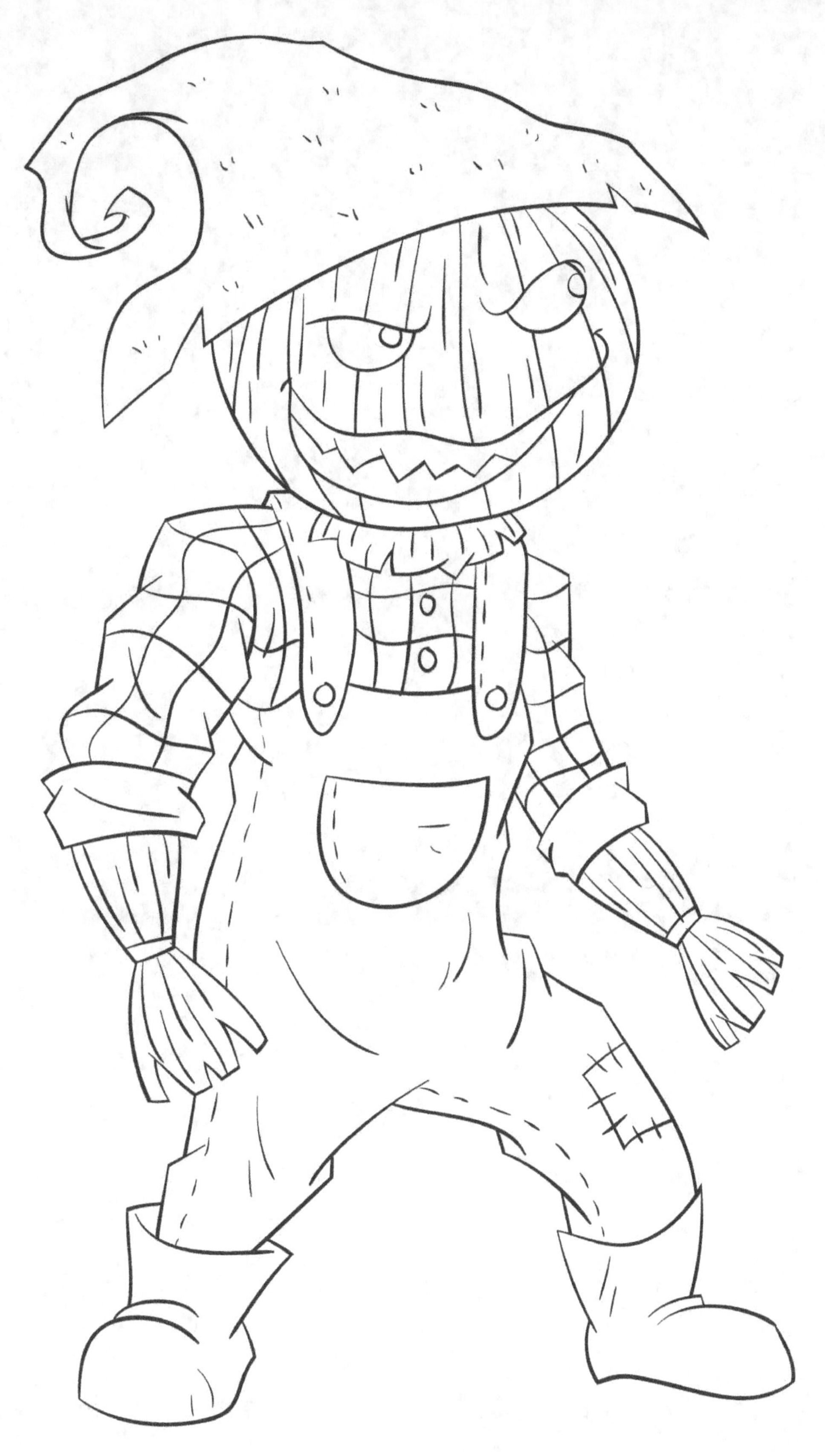

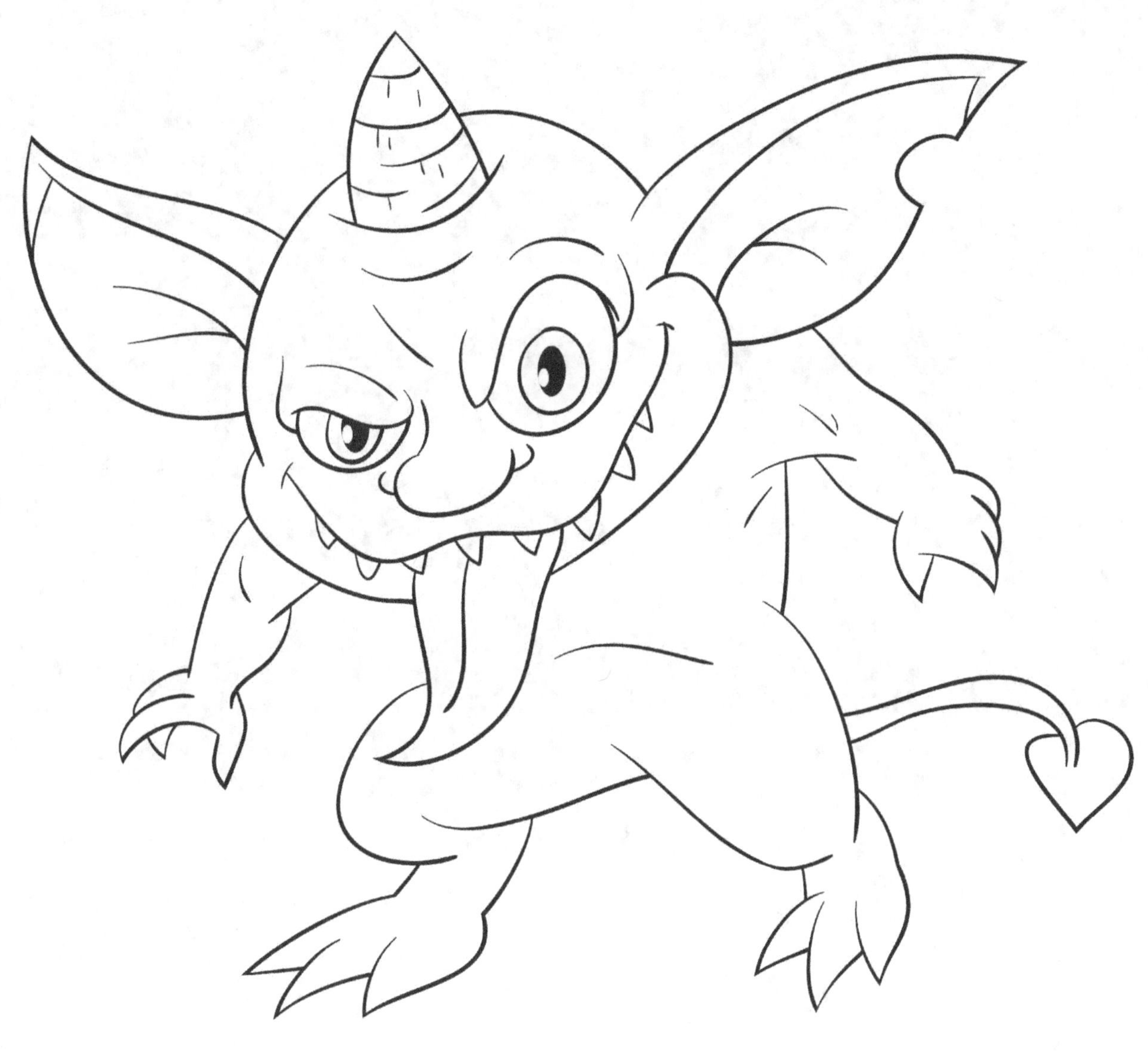

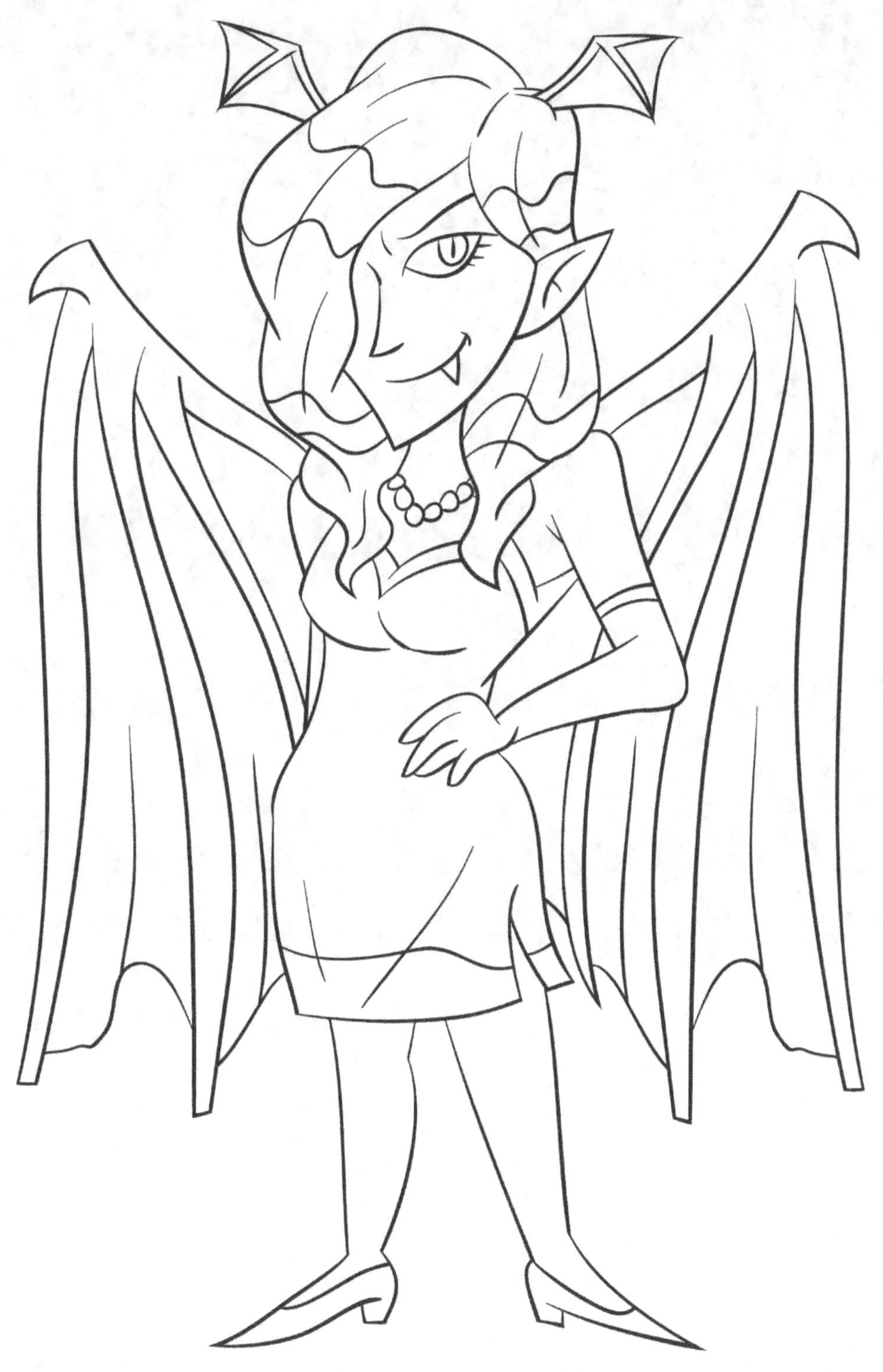

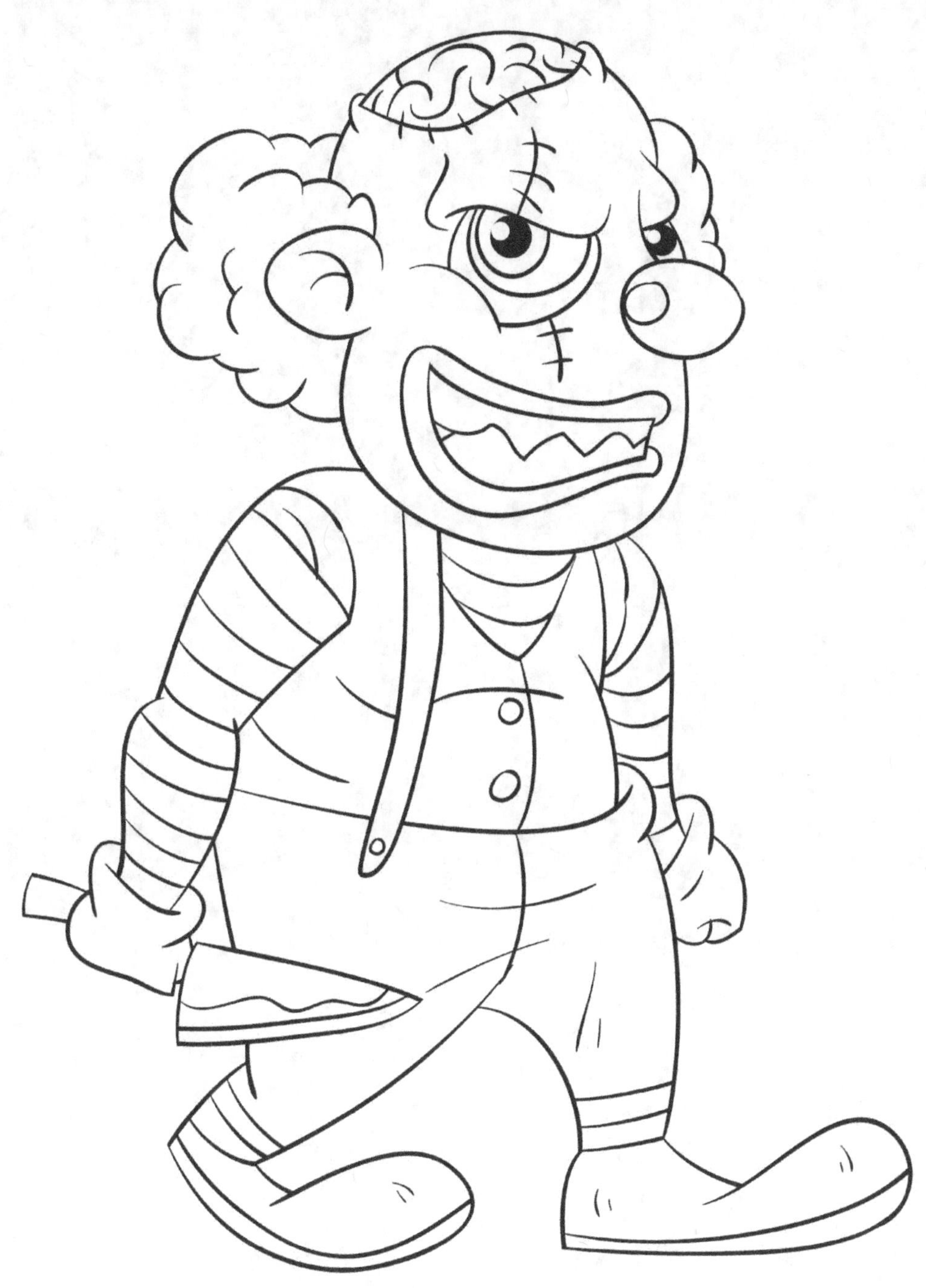

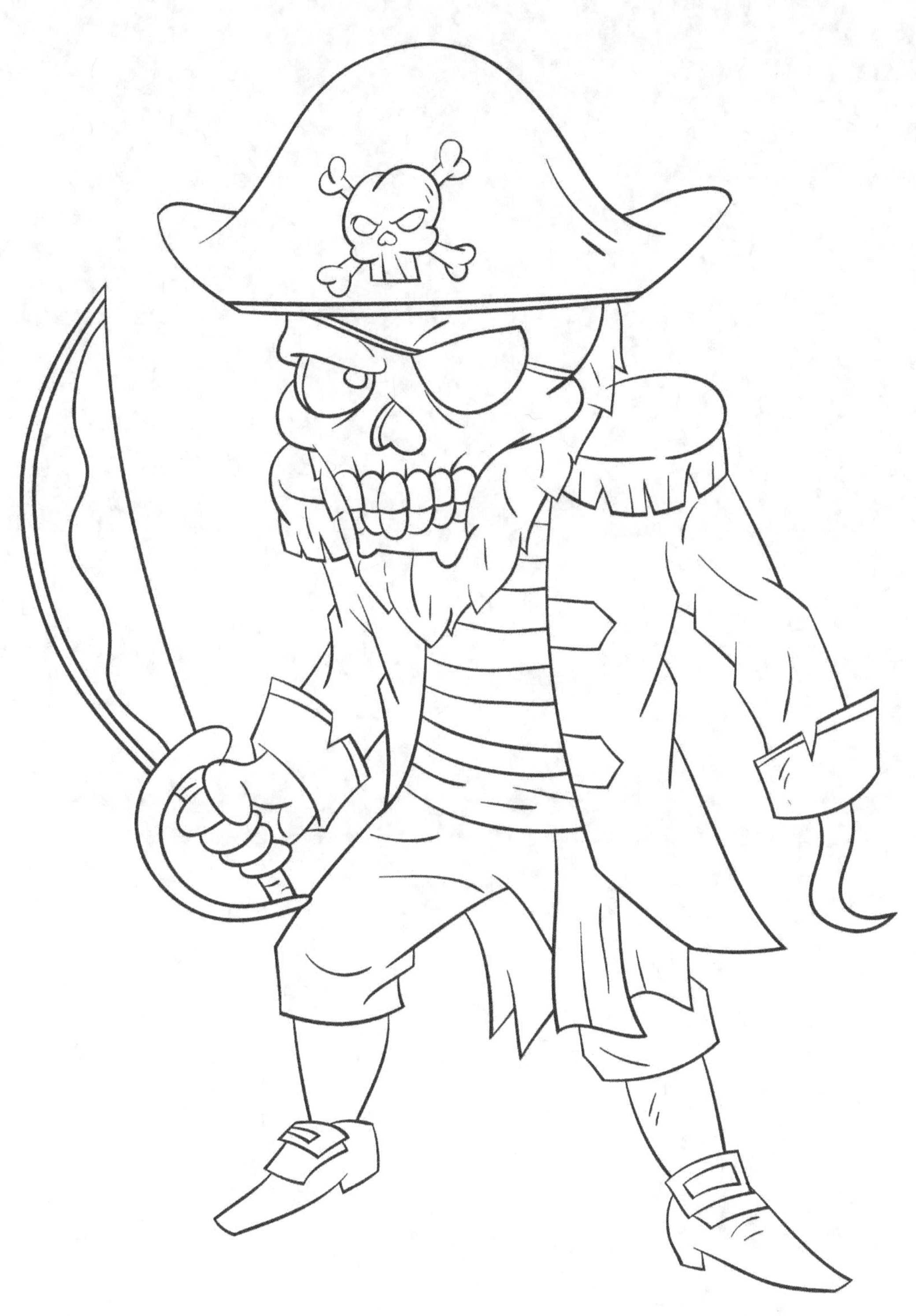

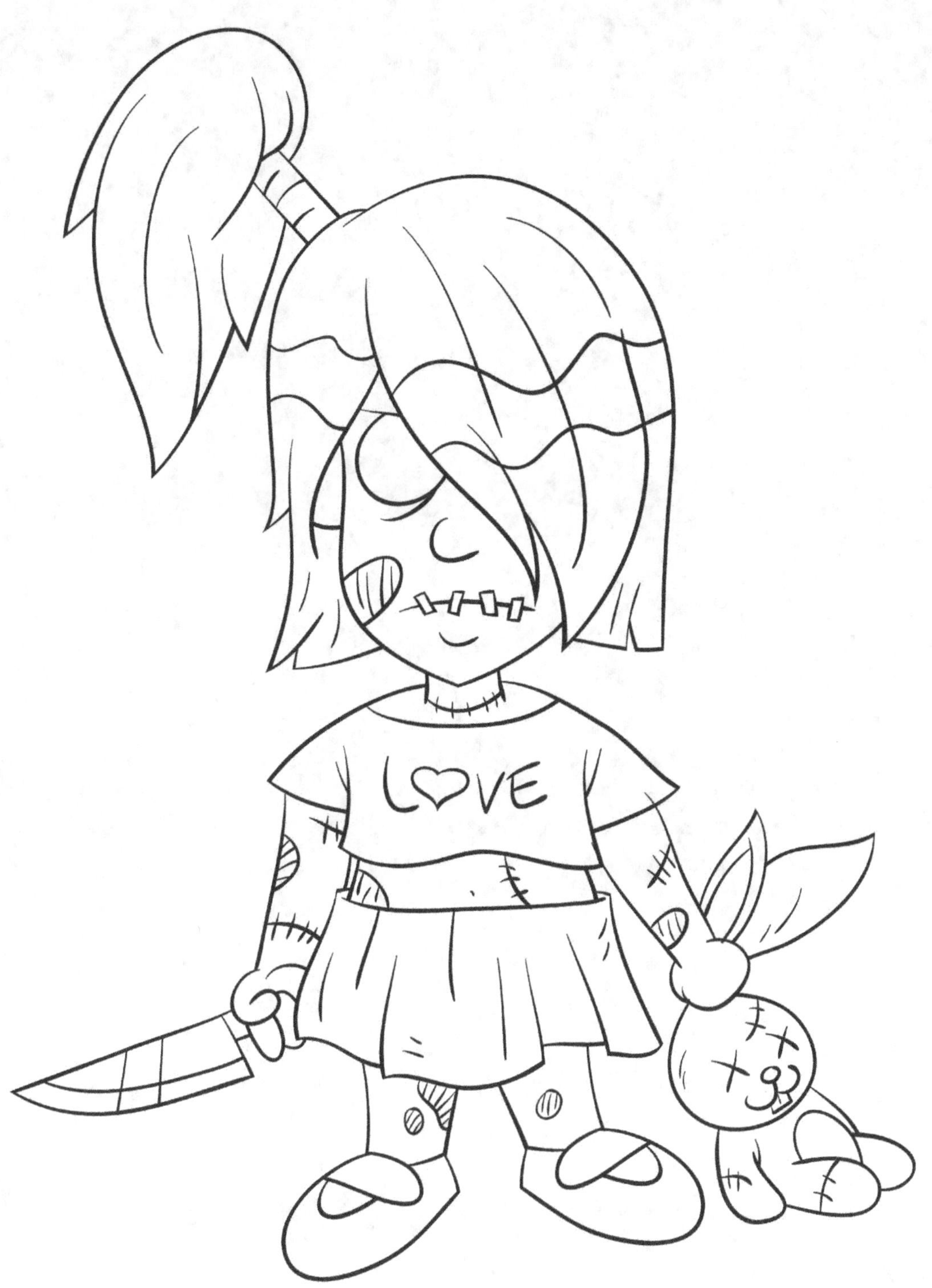

LOVE

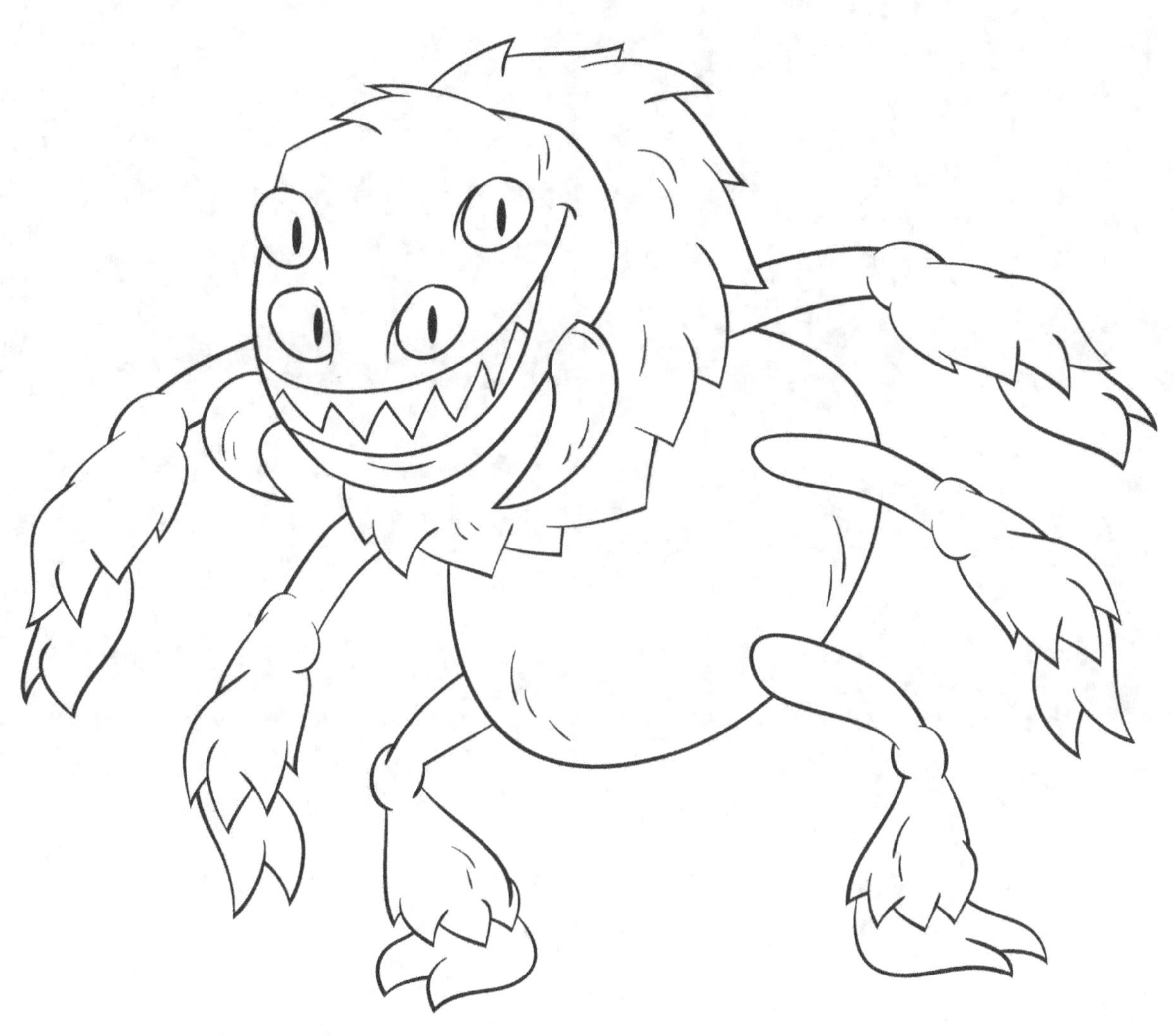

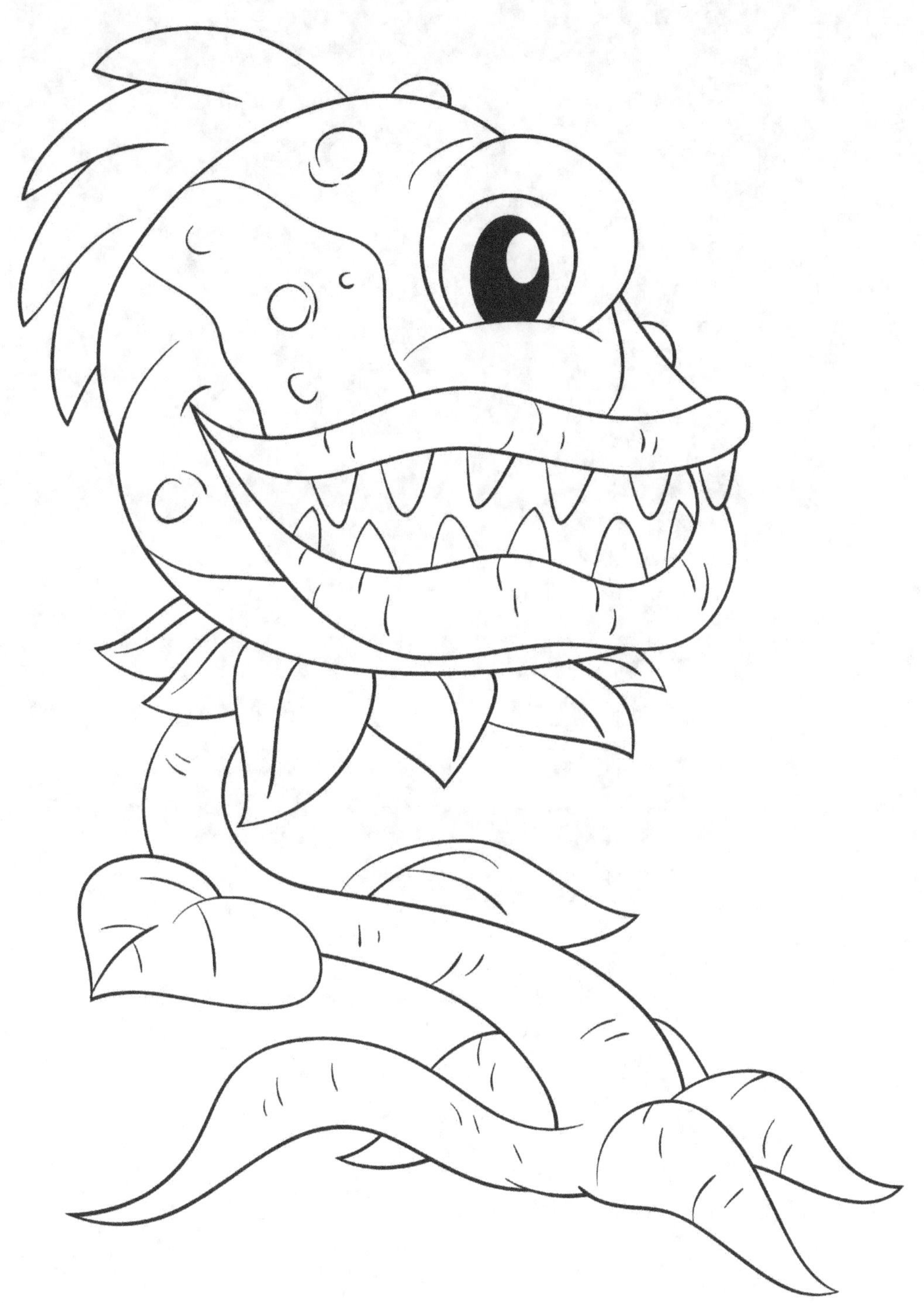

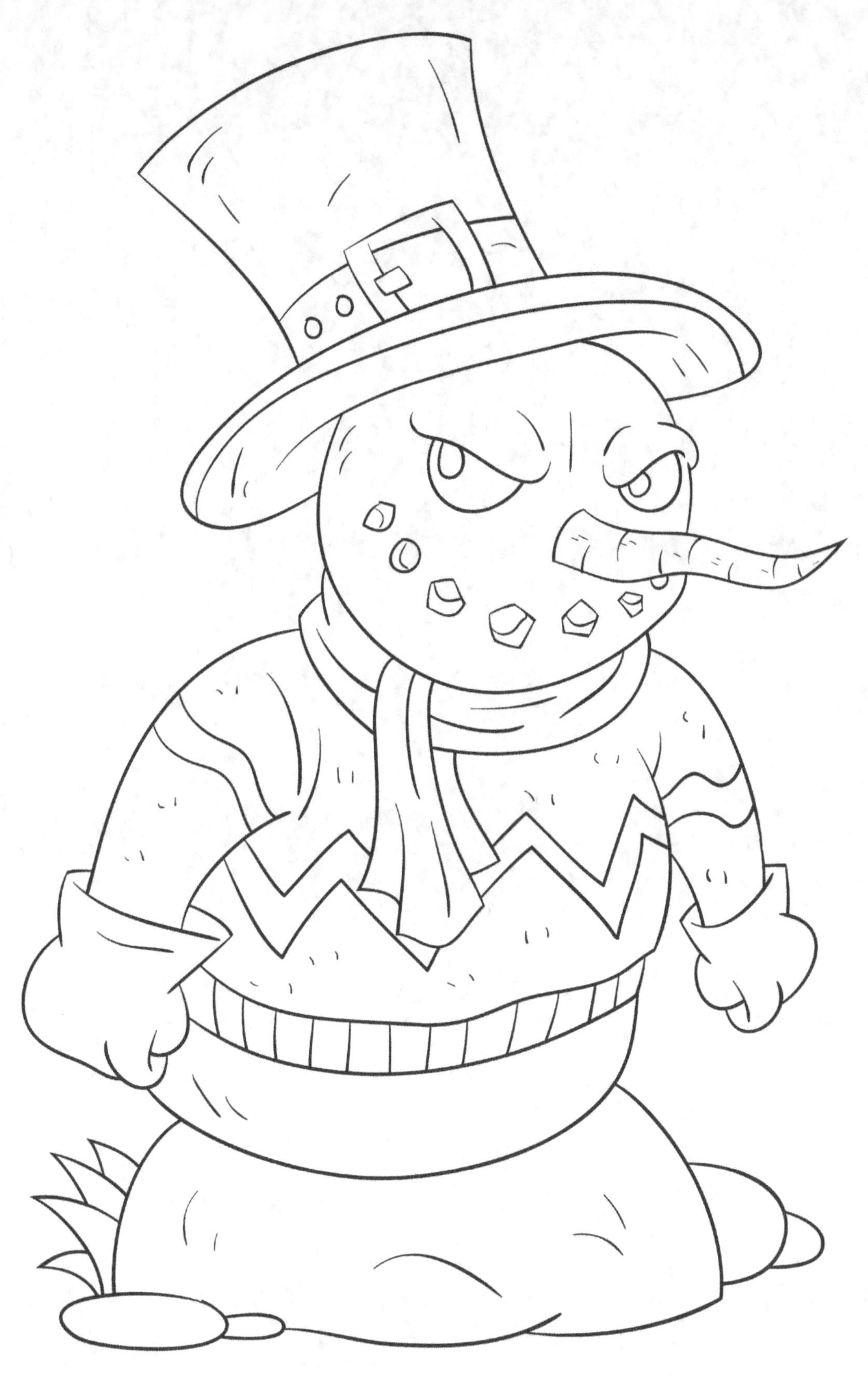

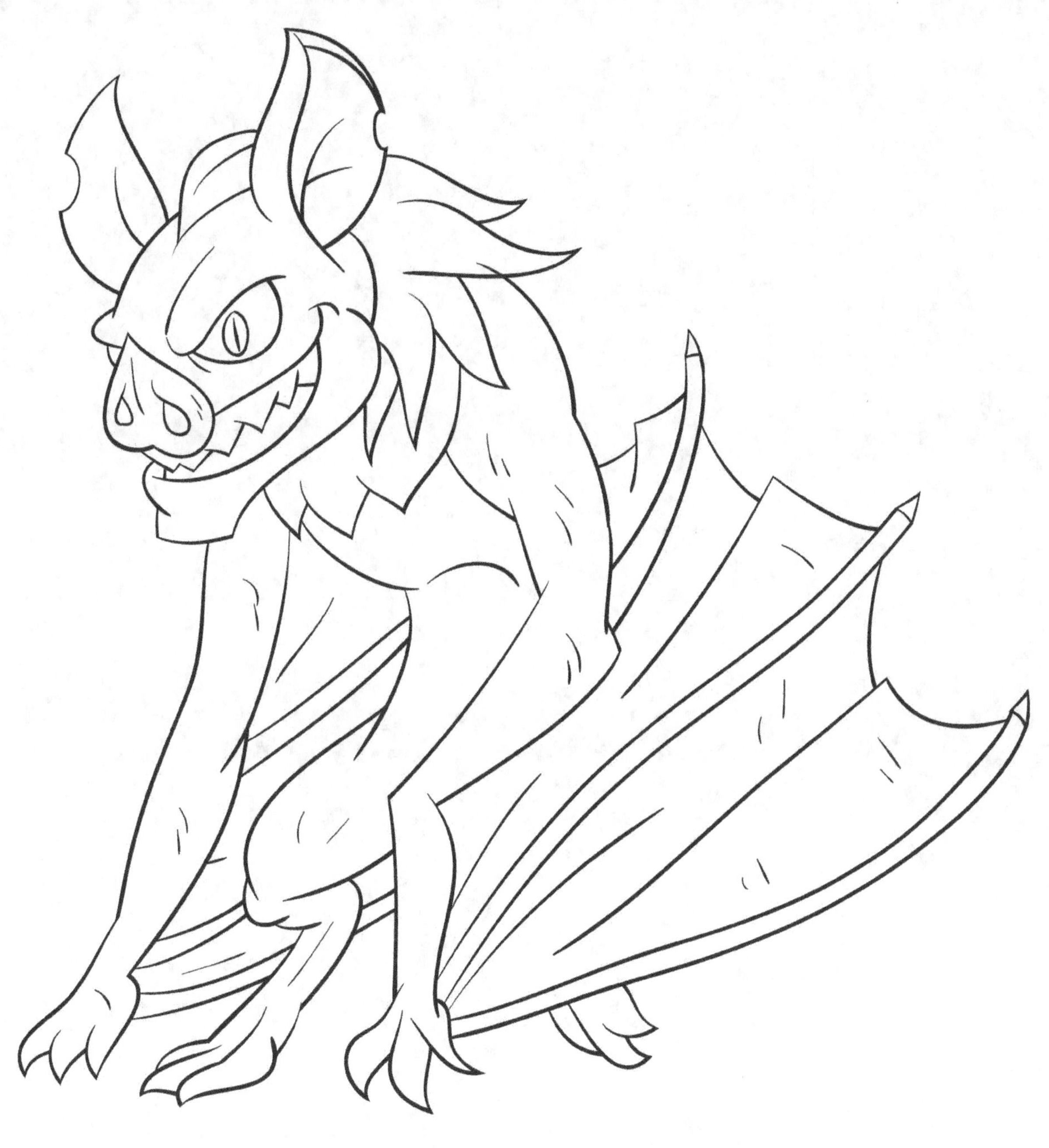

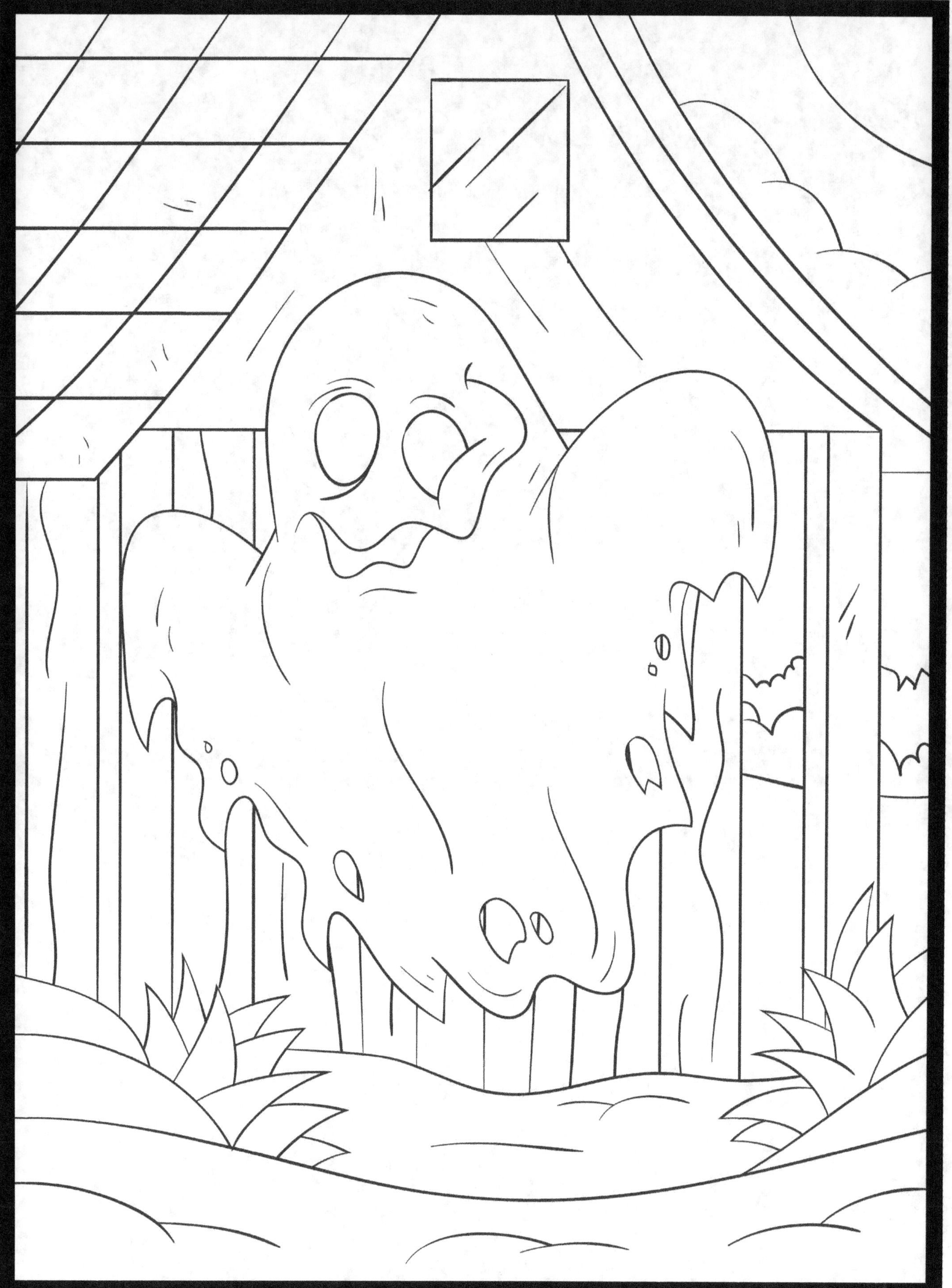

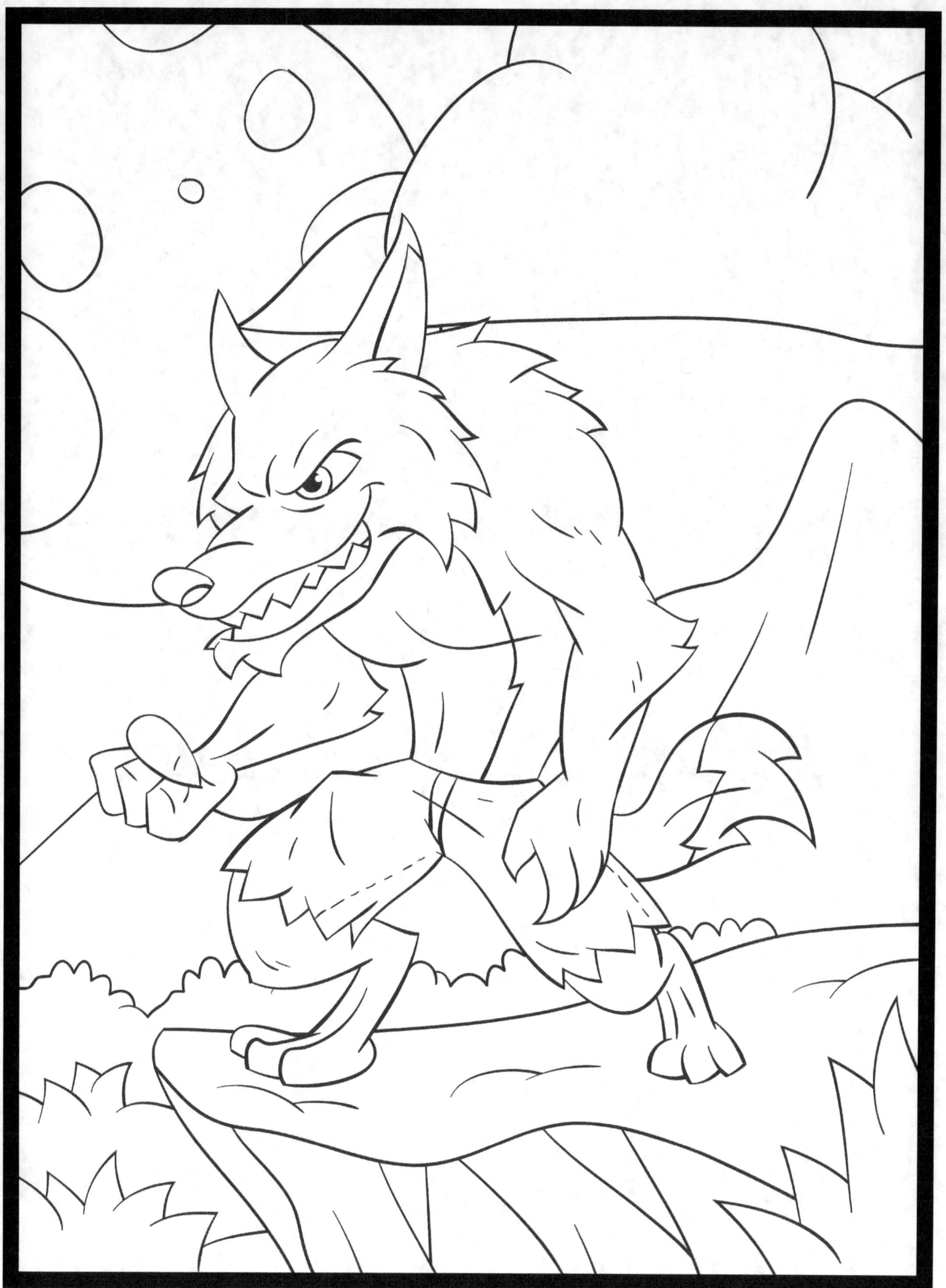

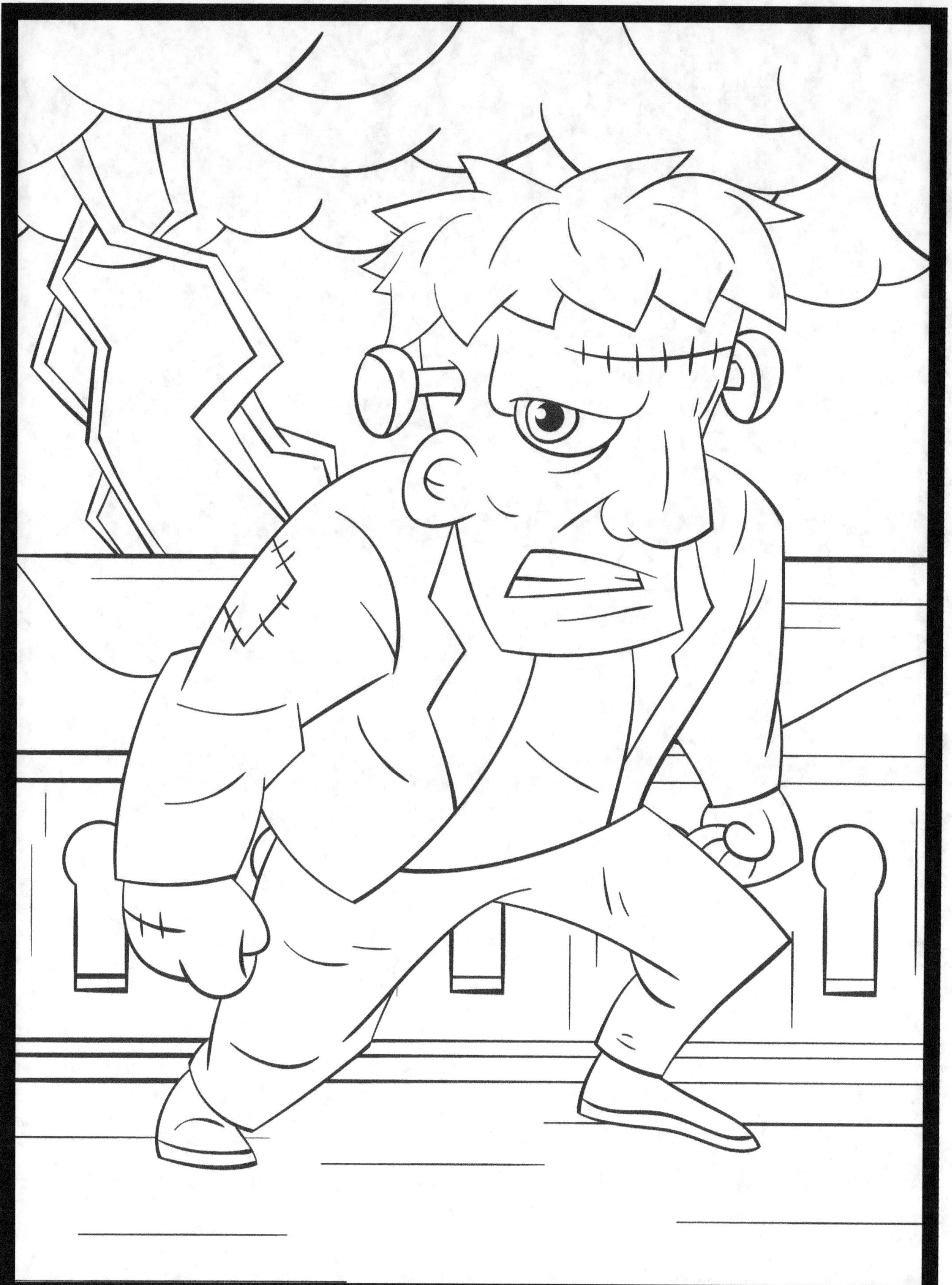

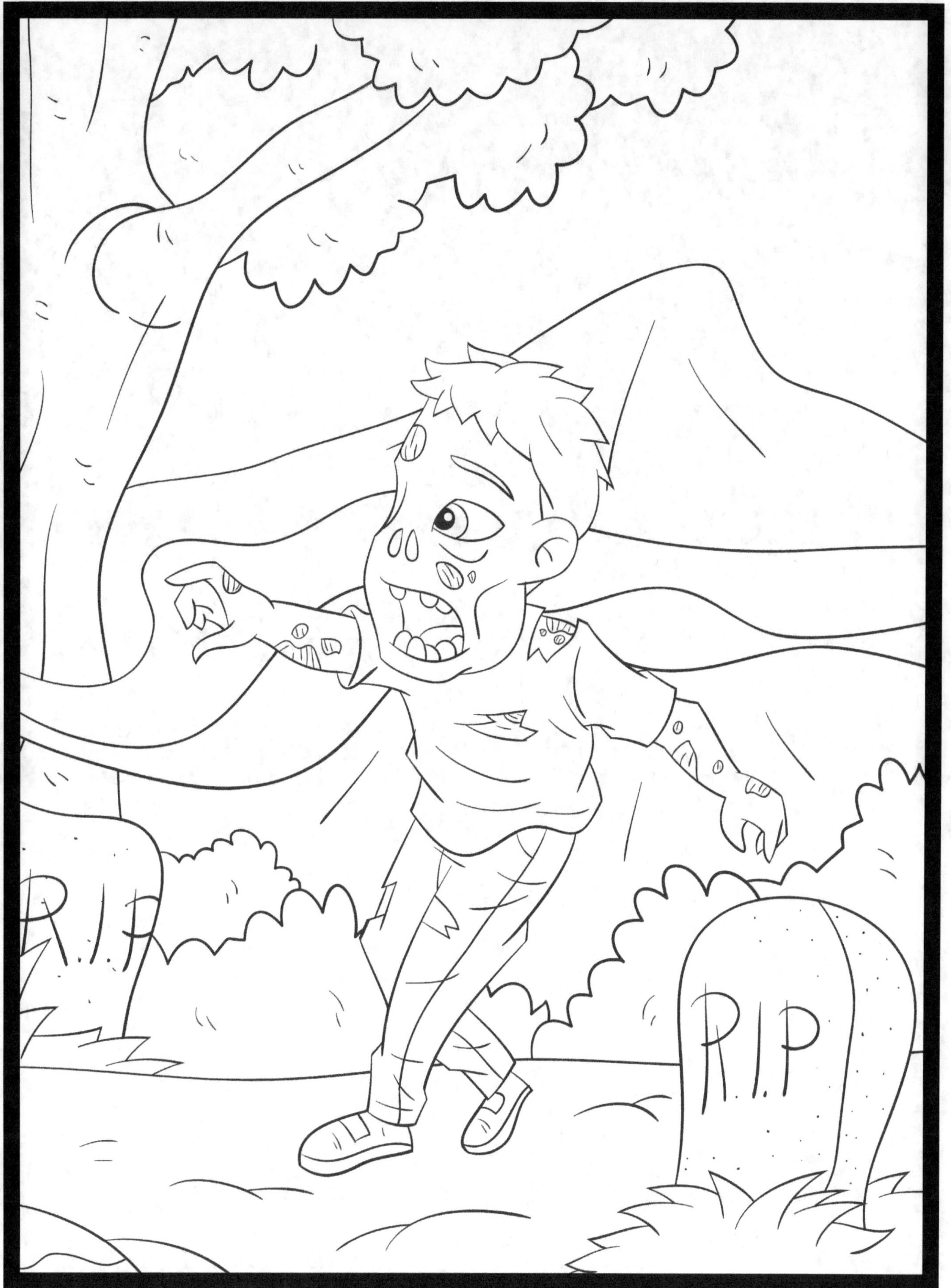

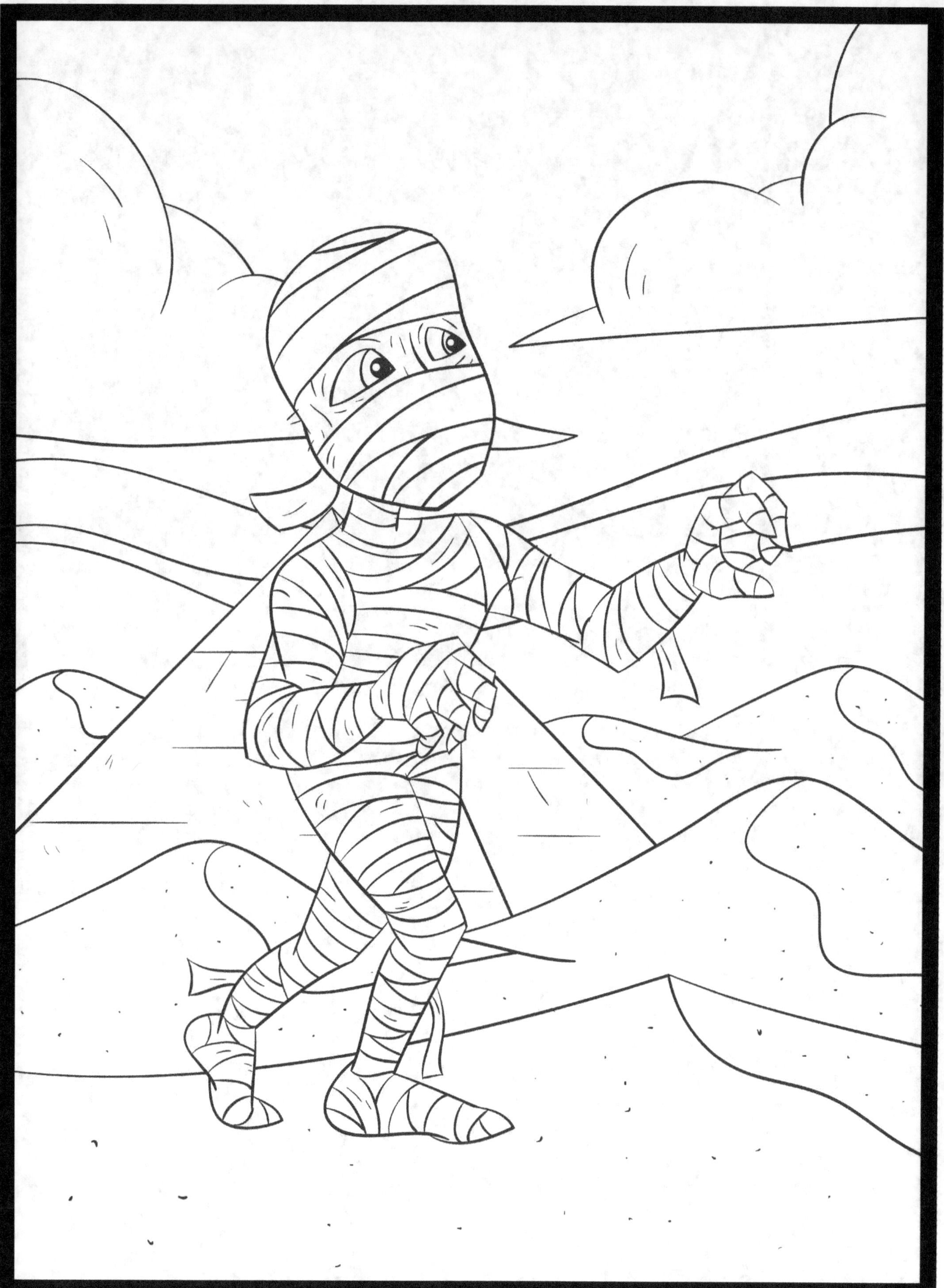

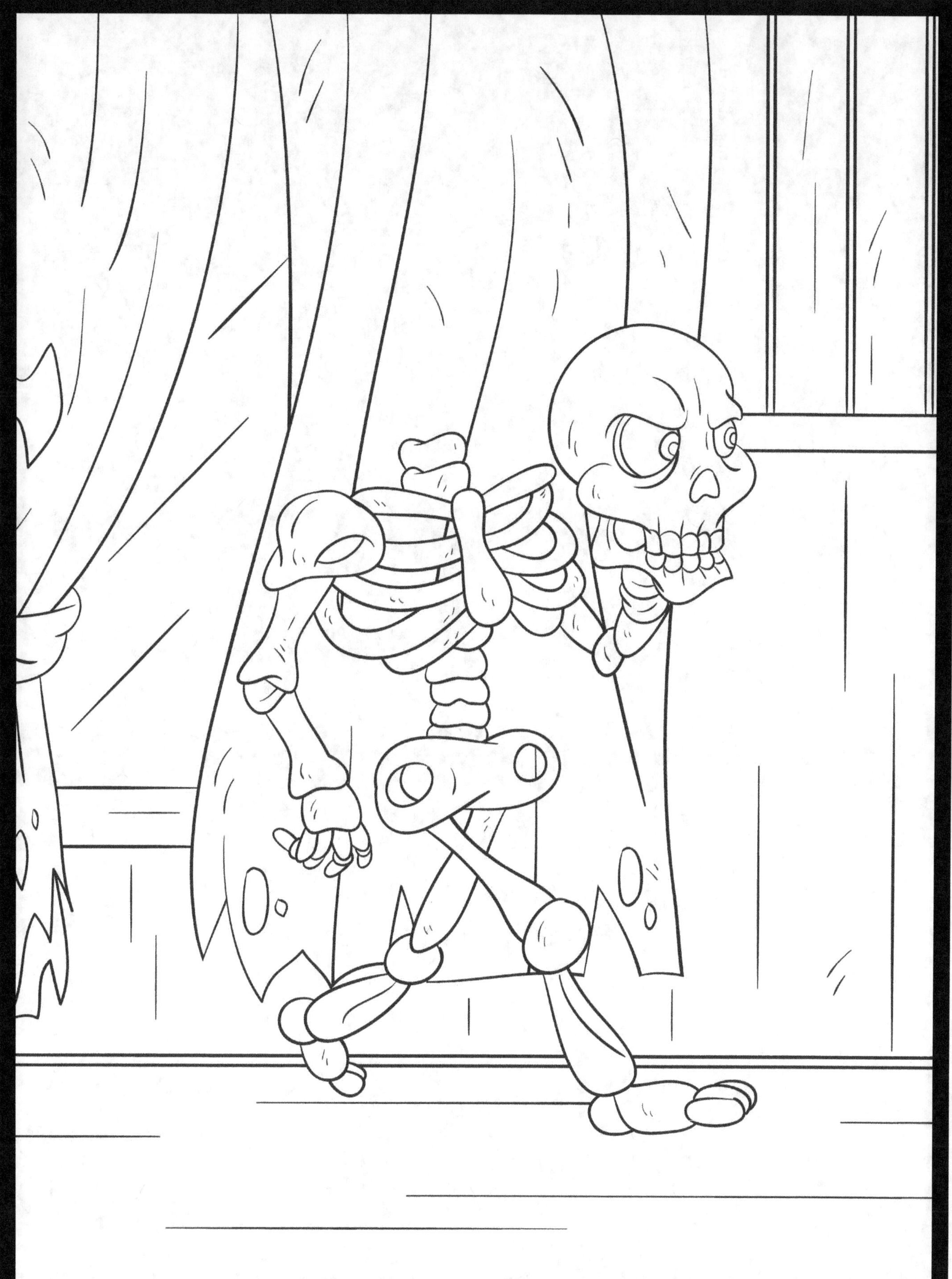

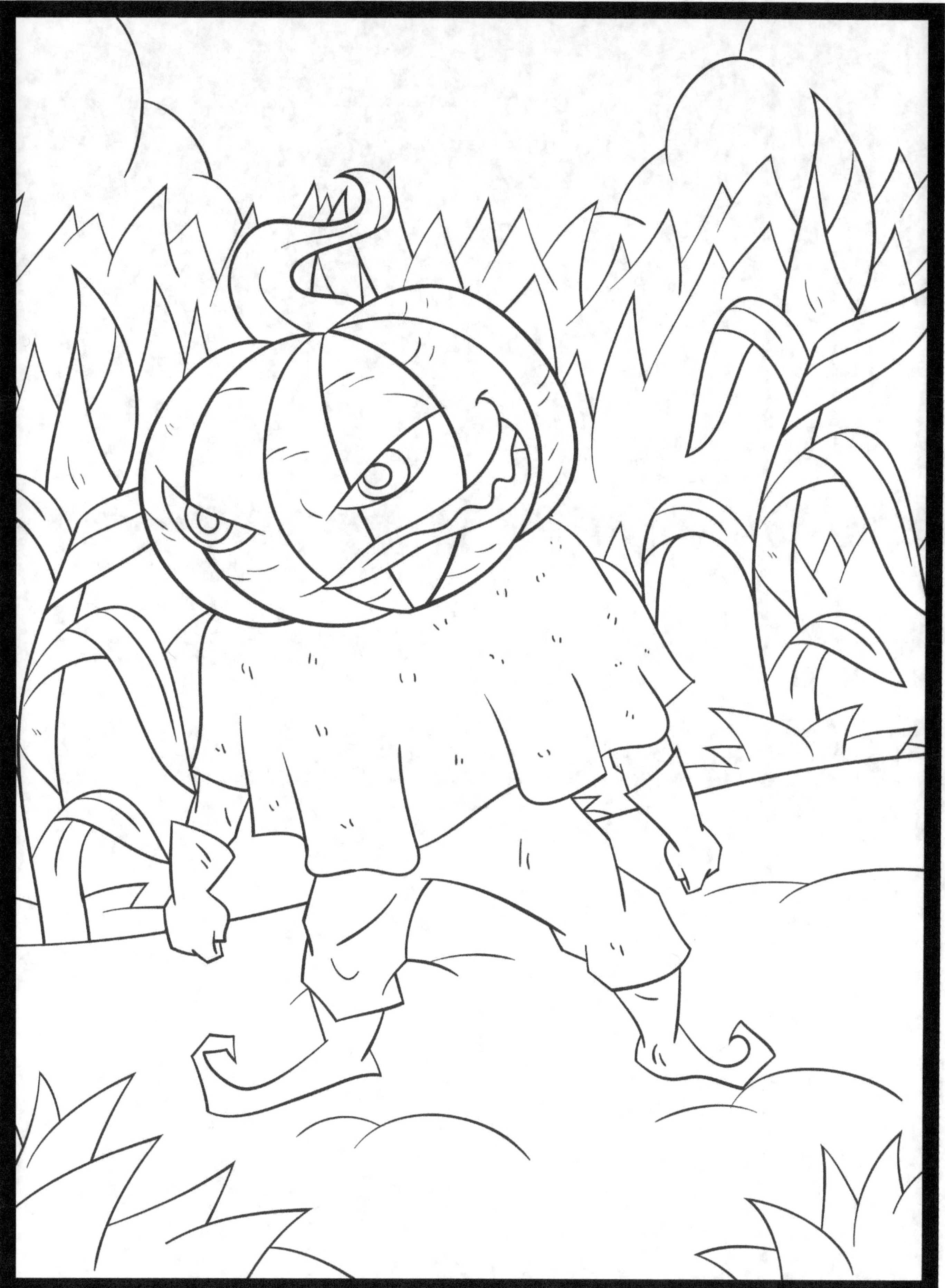

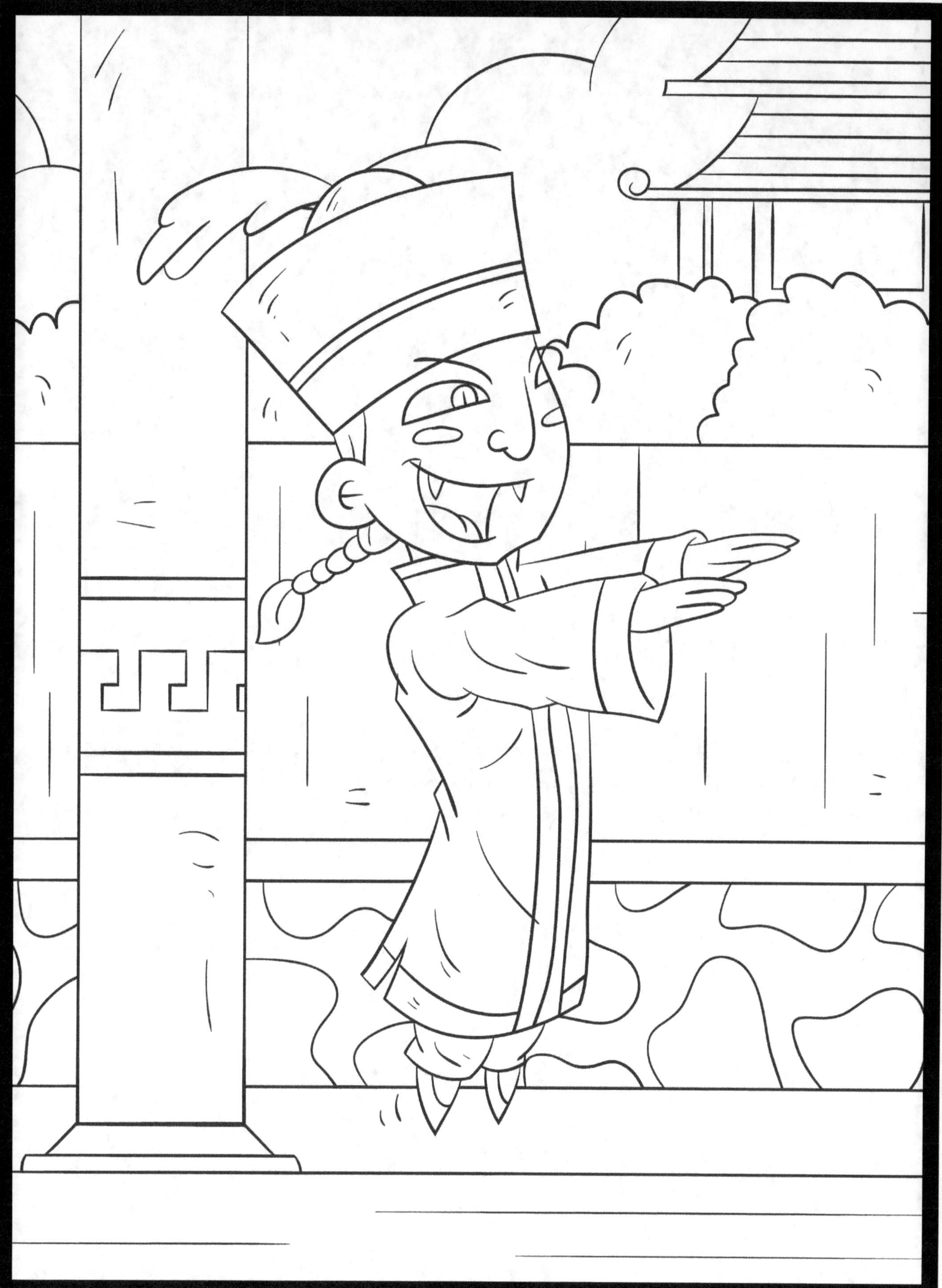

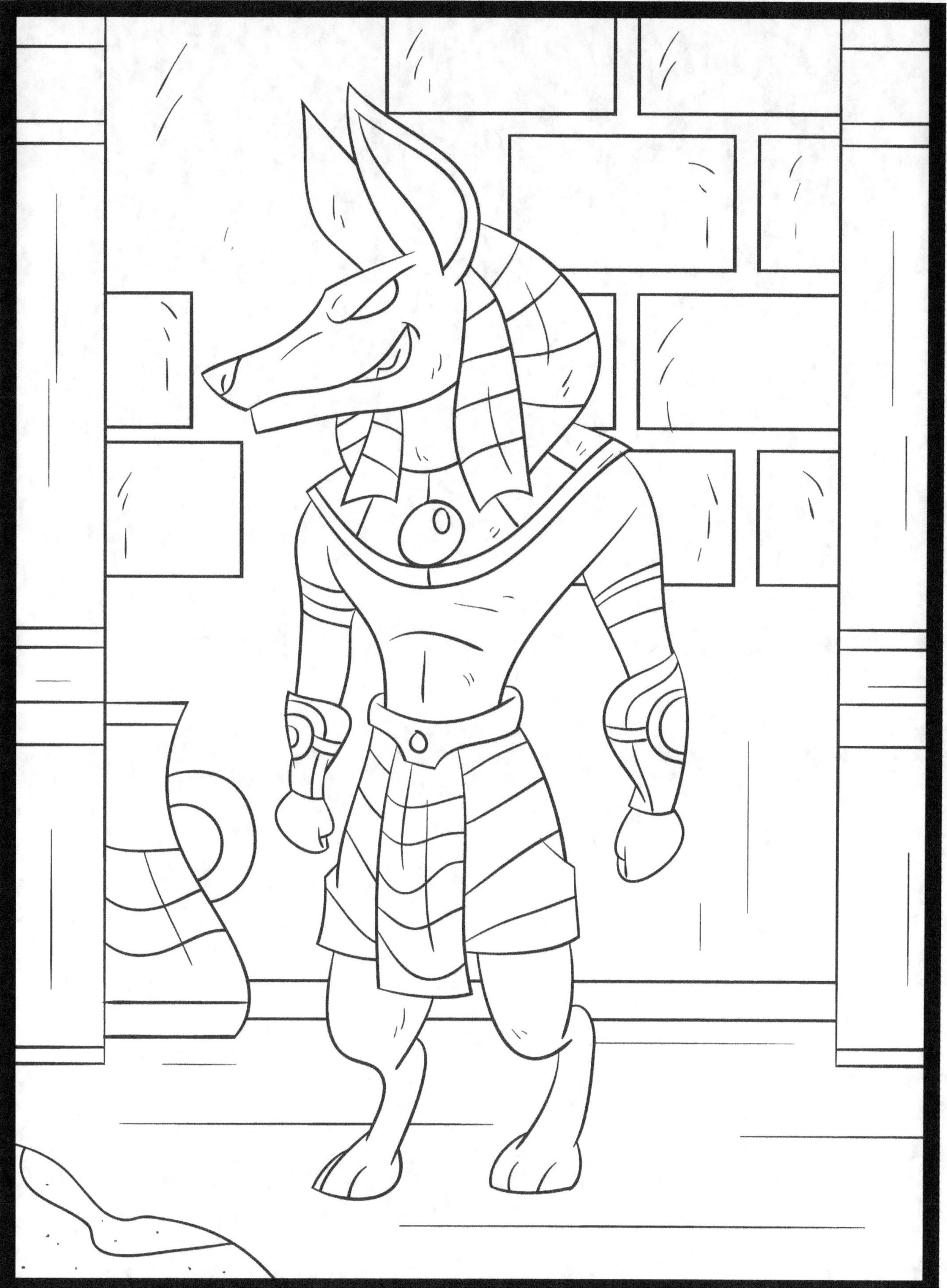

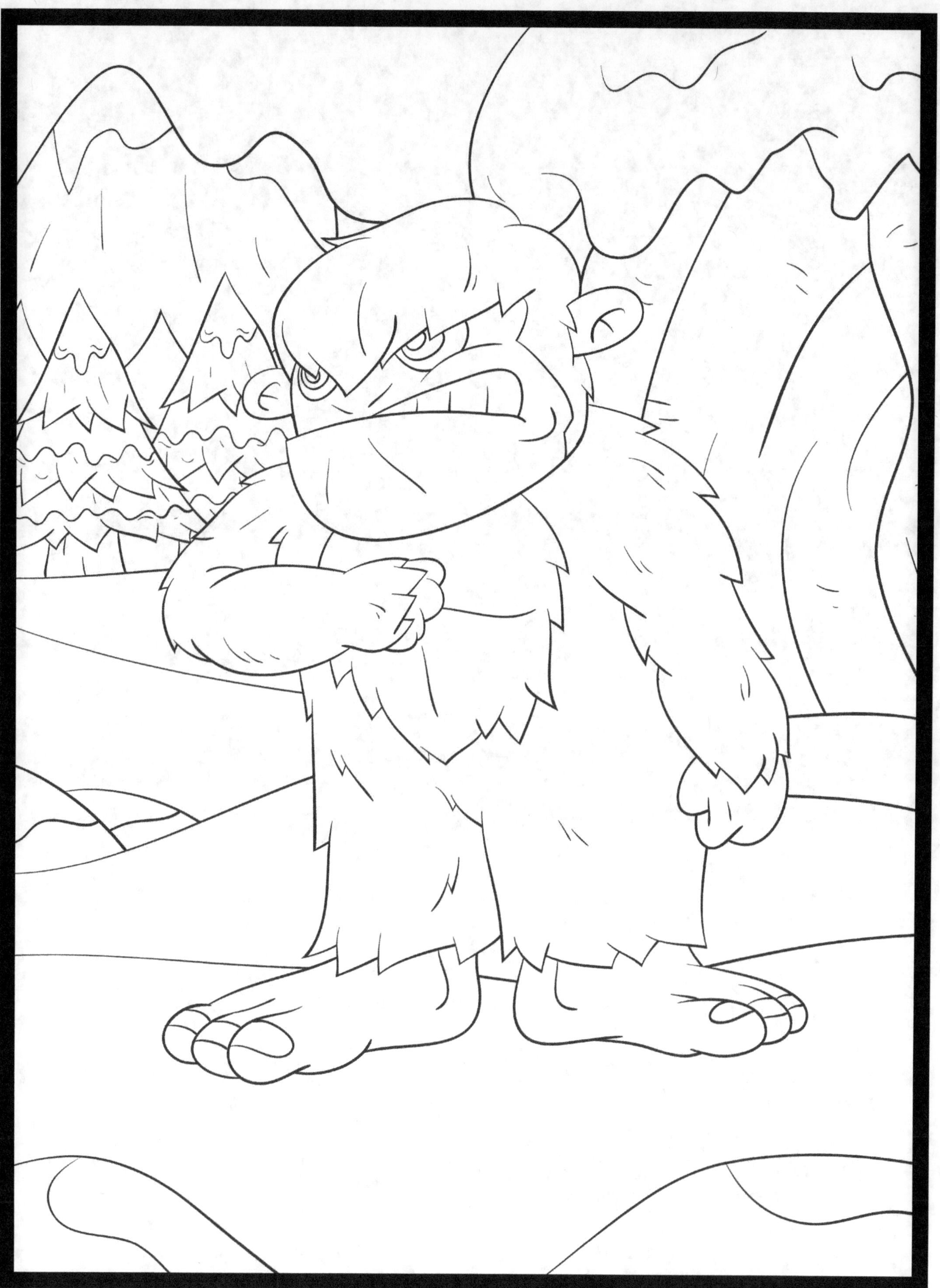

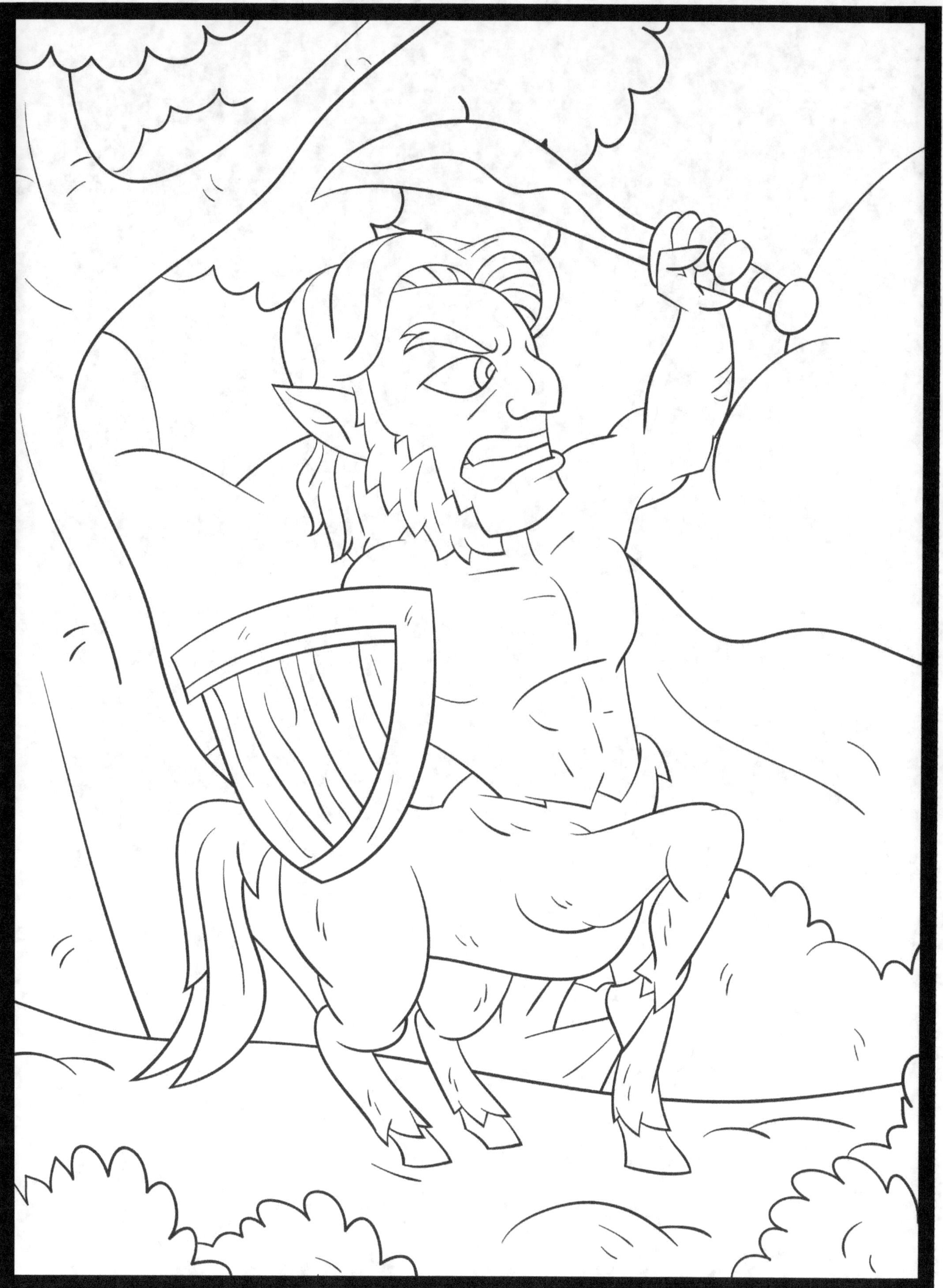

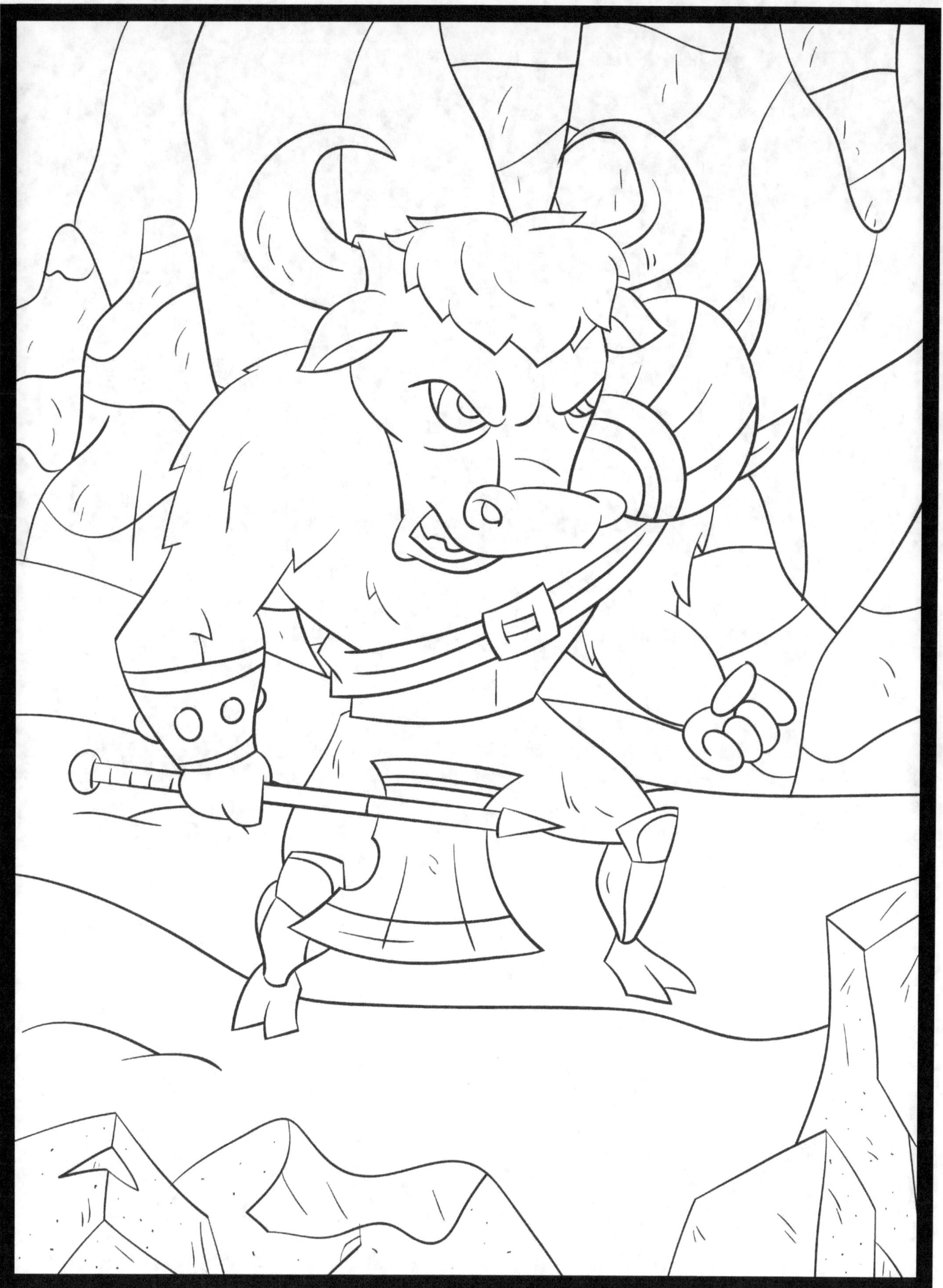

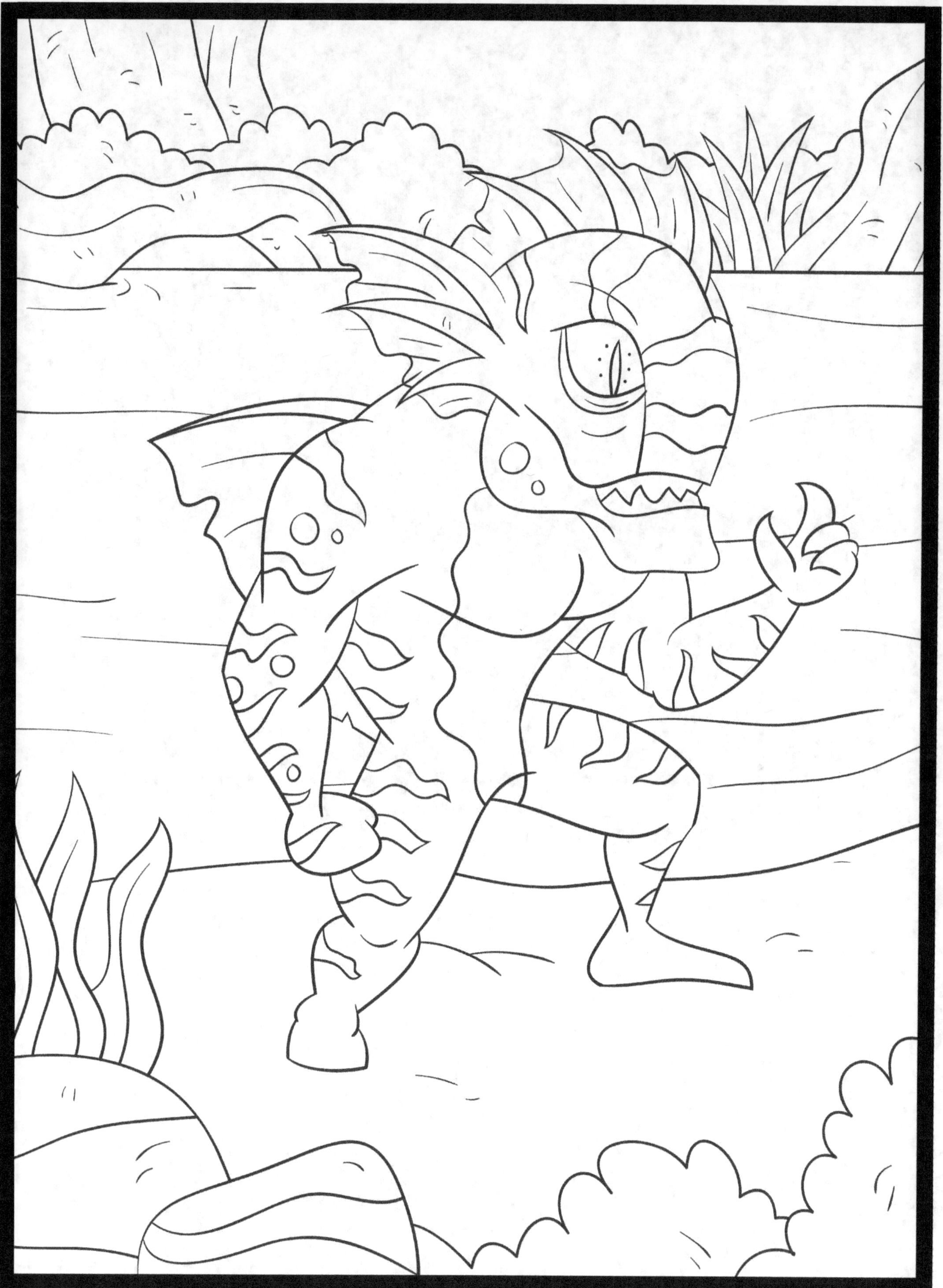

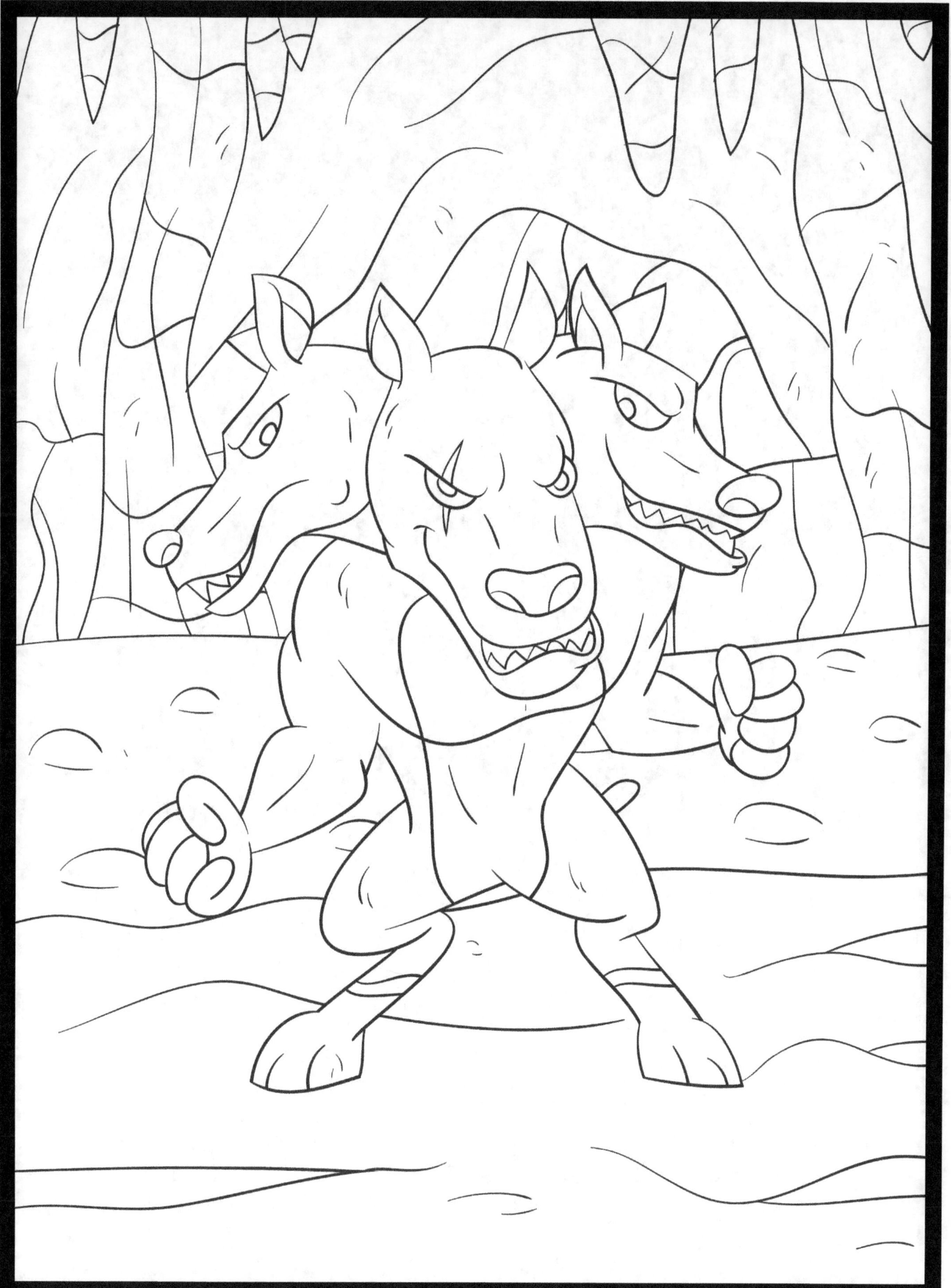

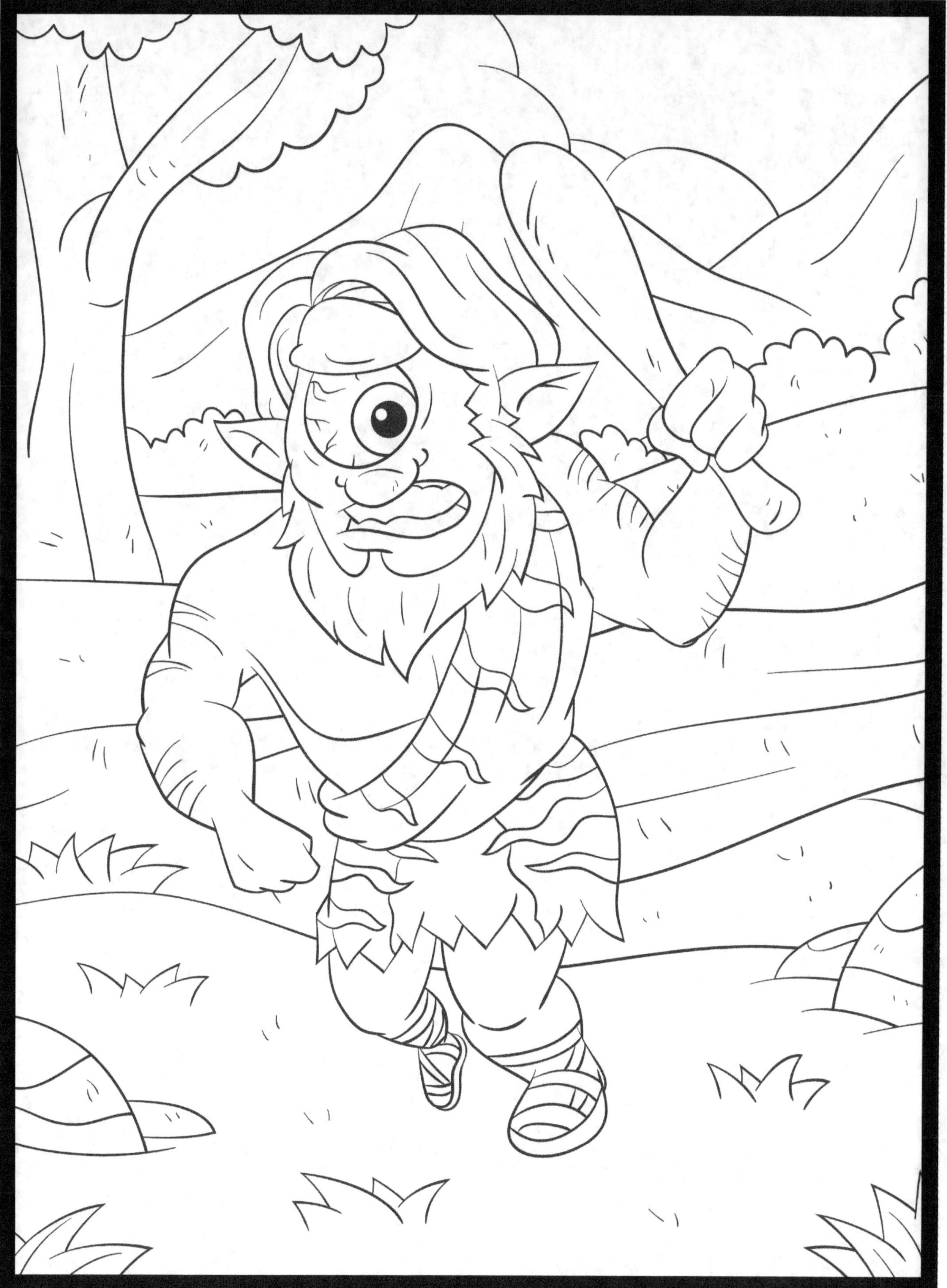

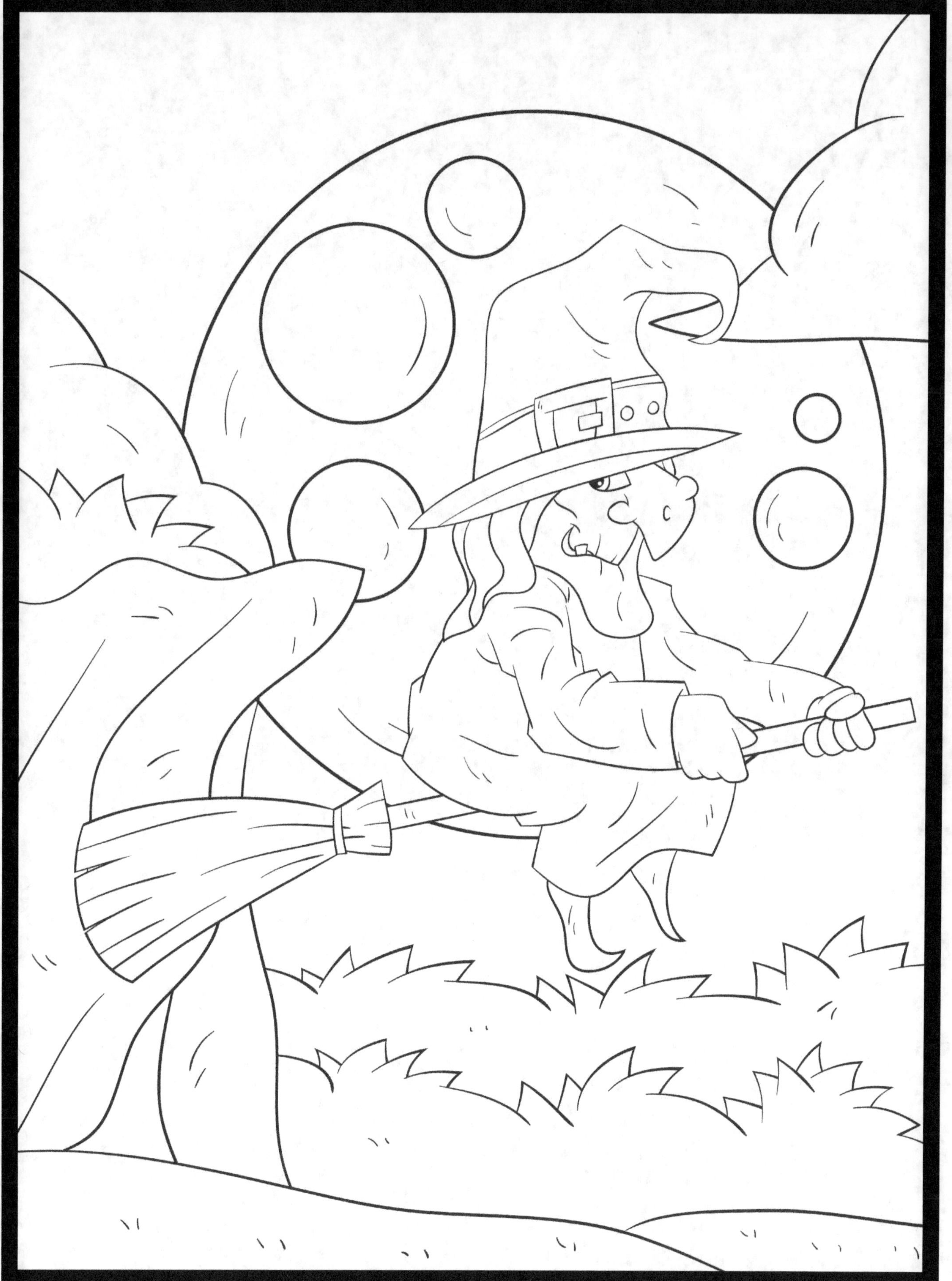

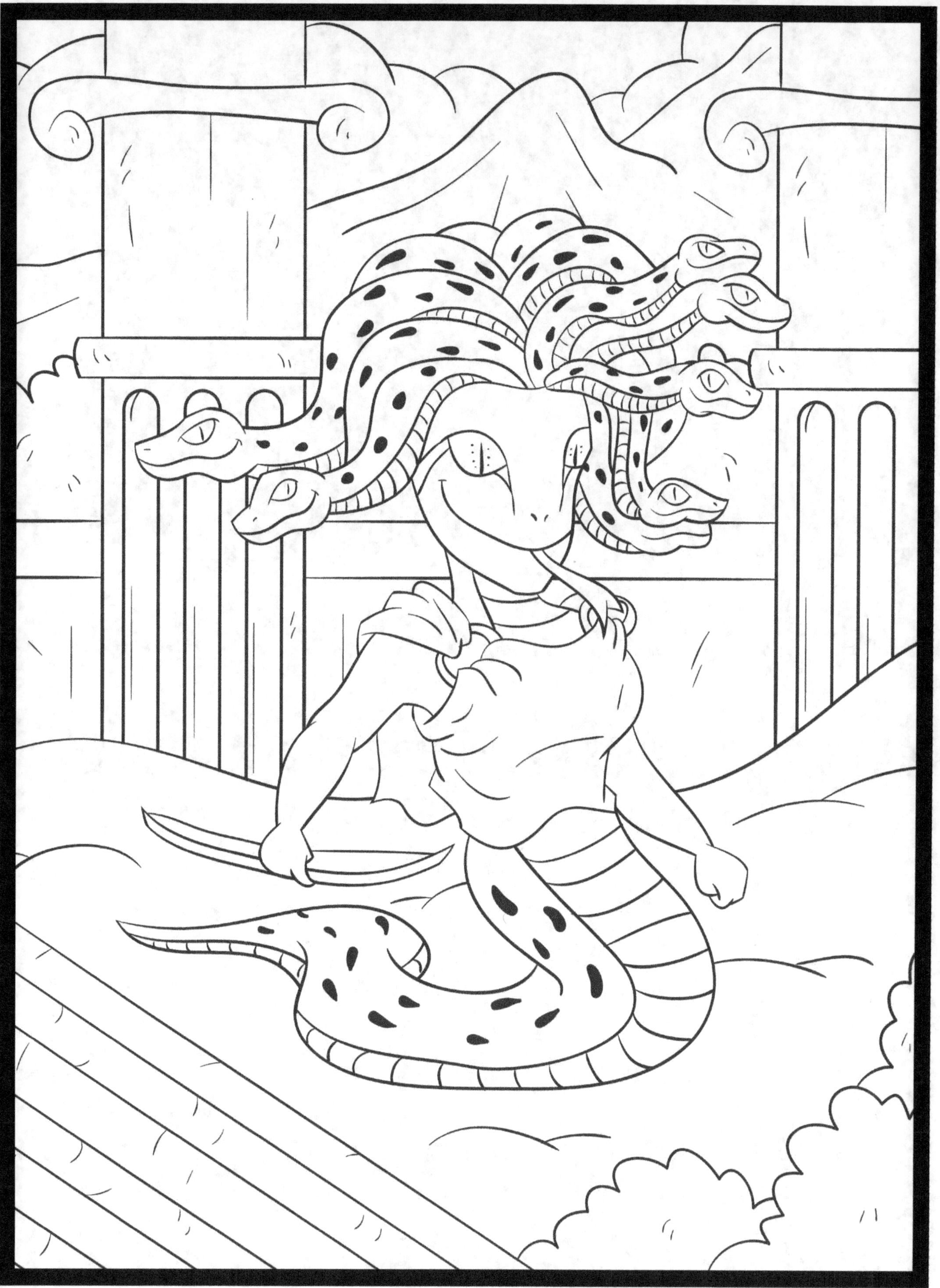

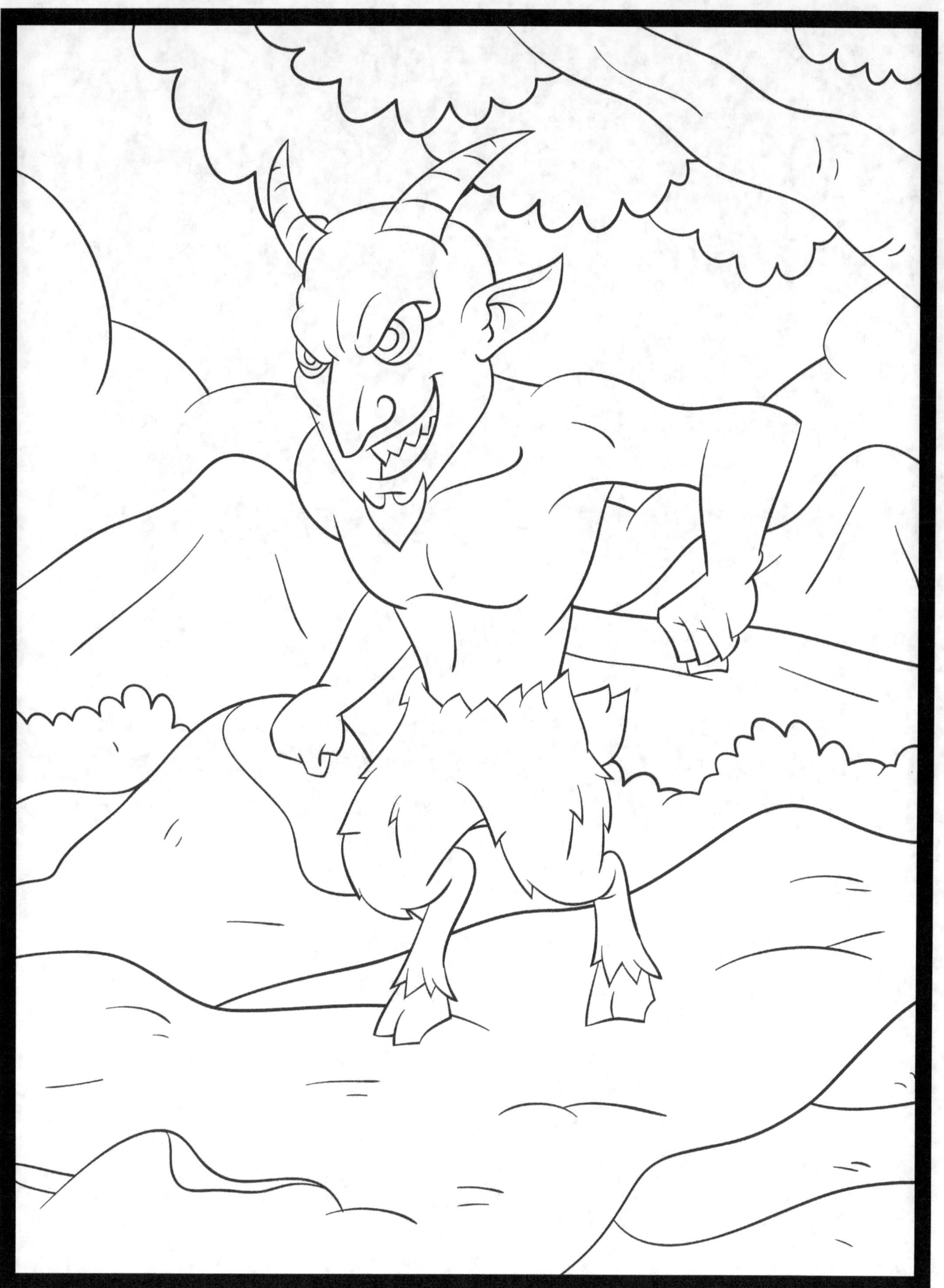

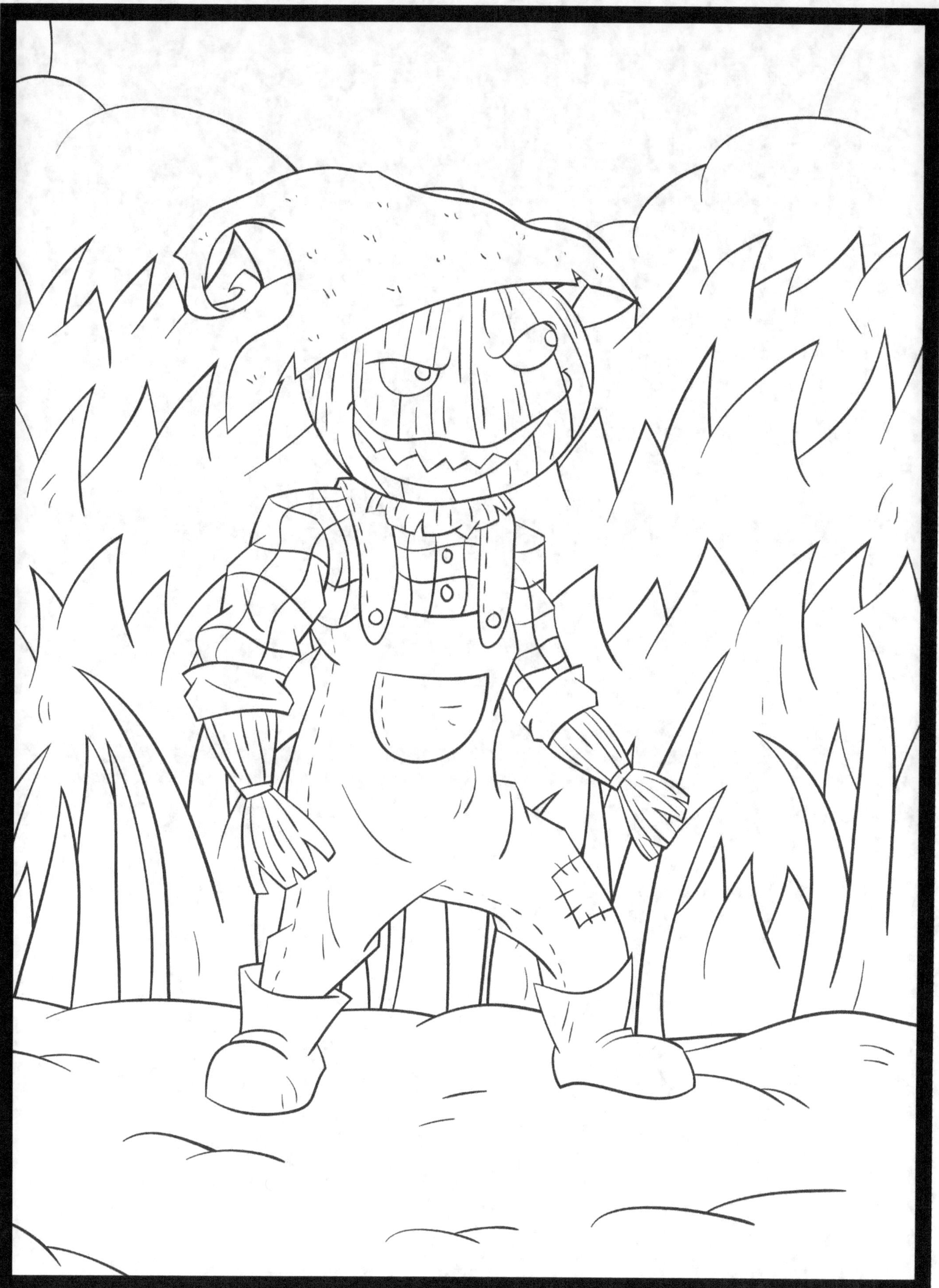

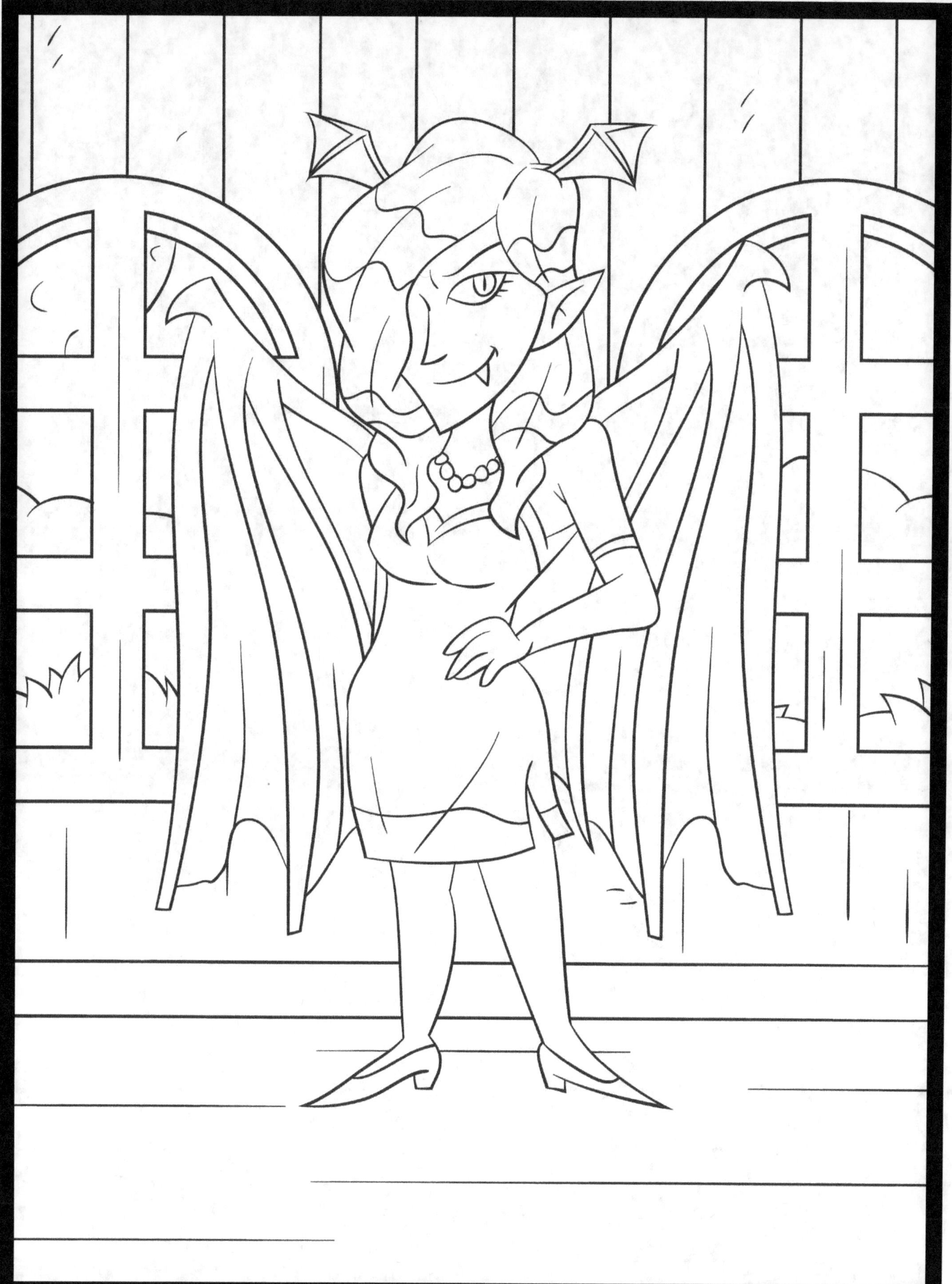

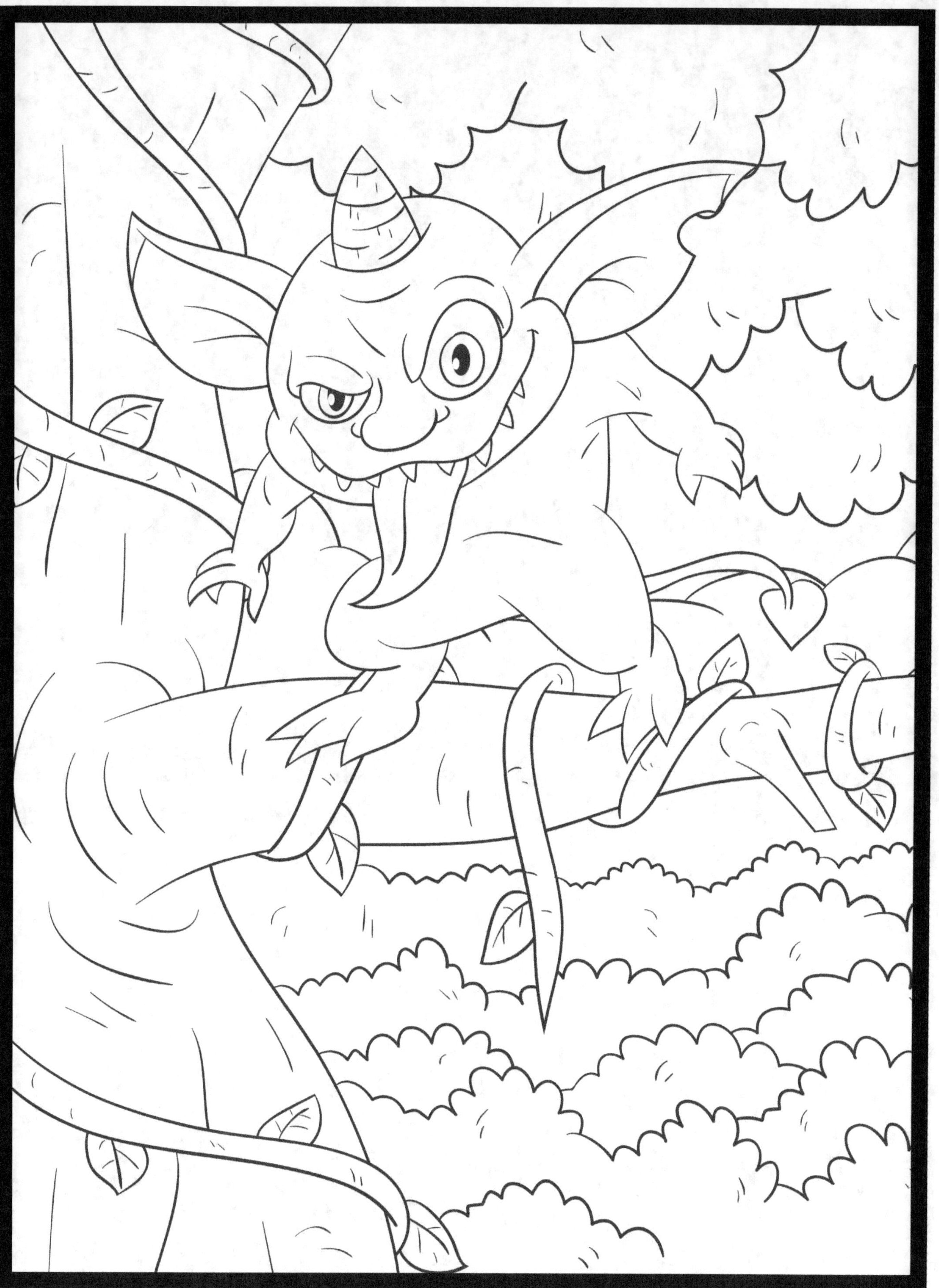

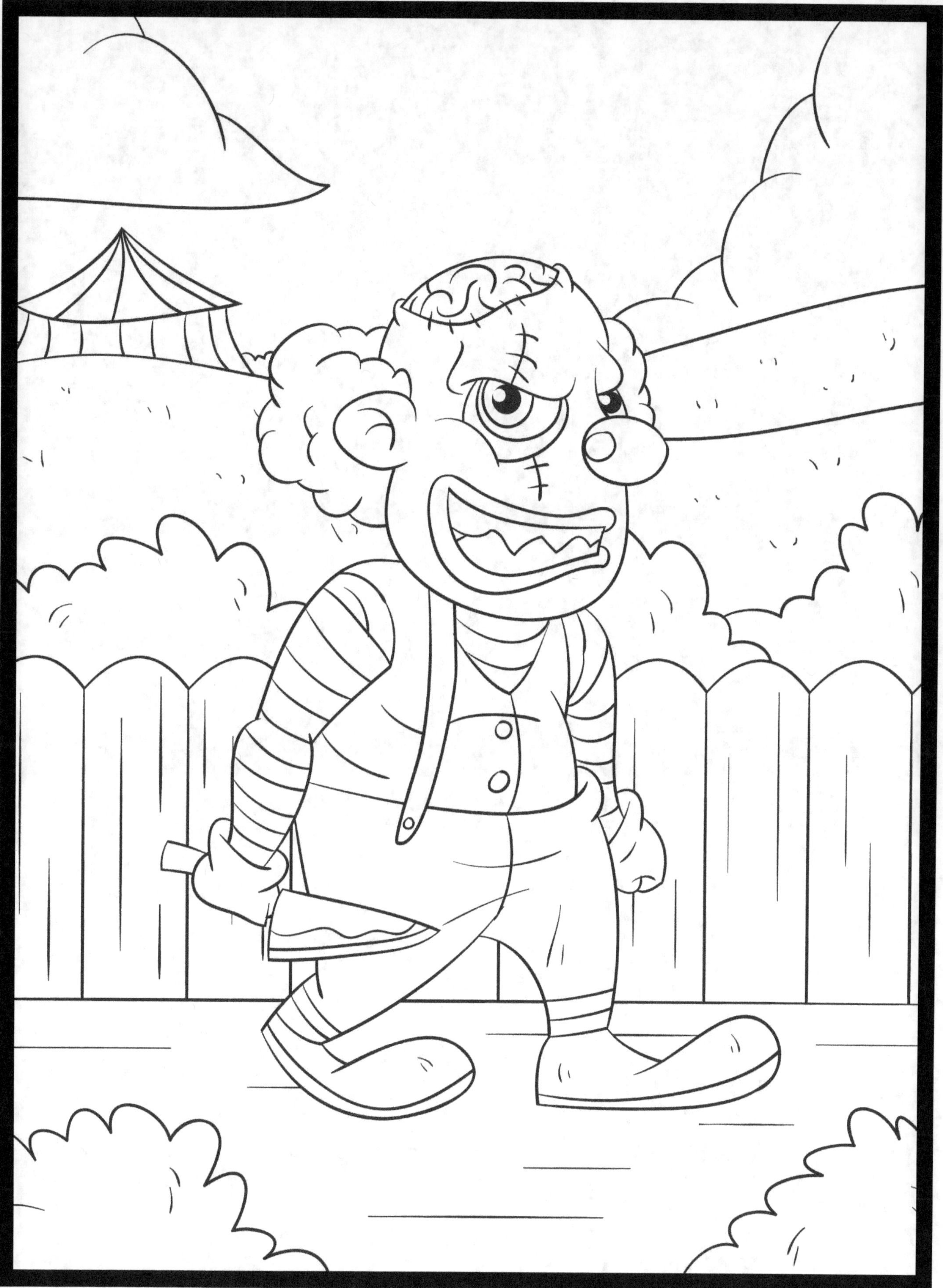

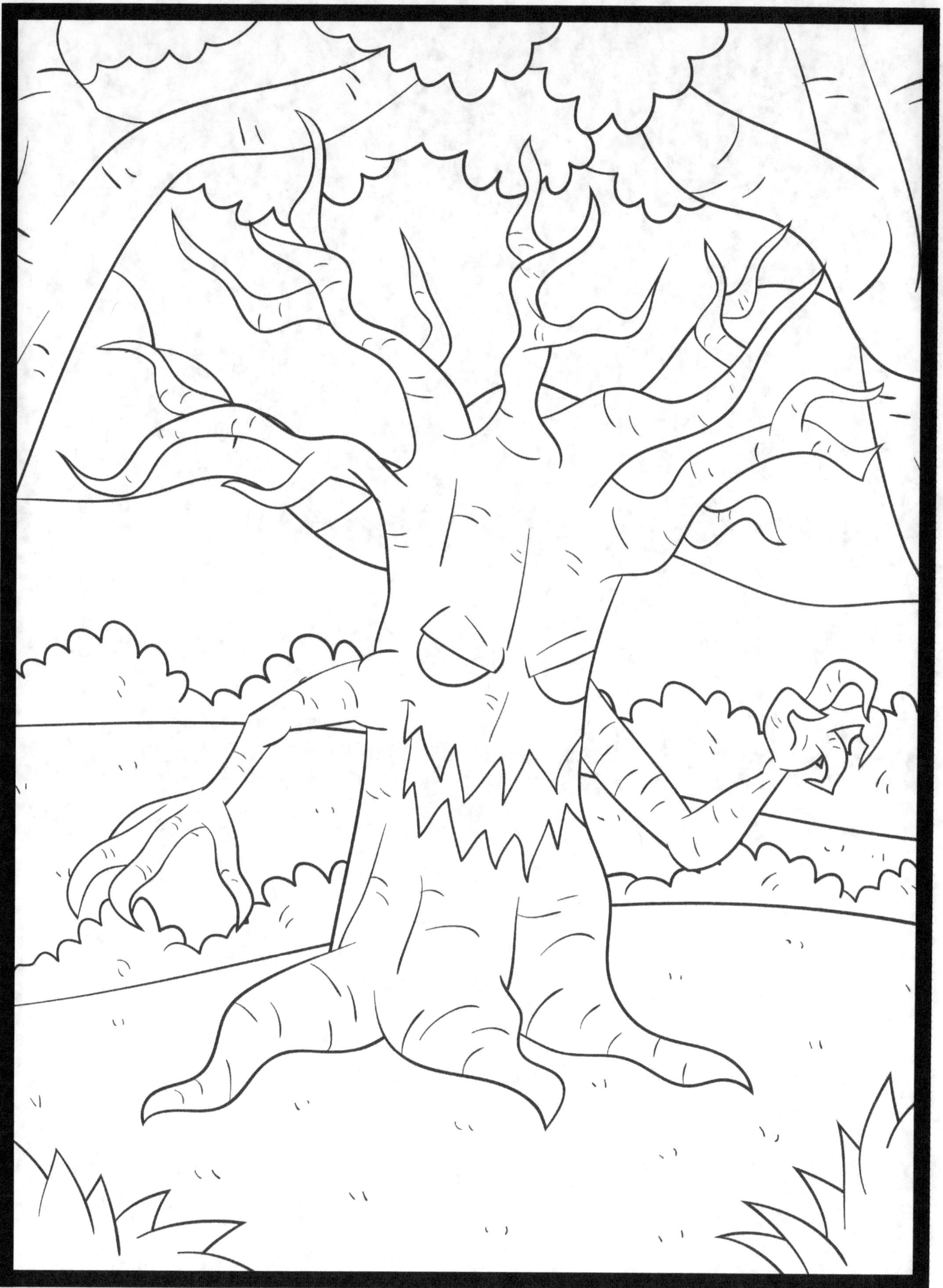

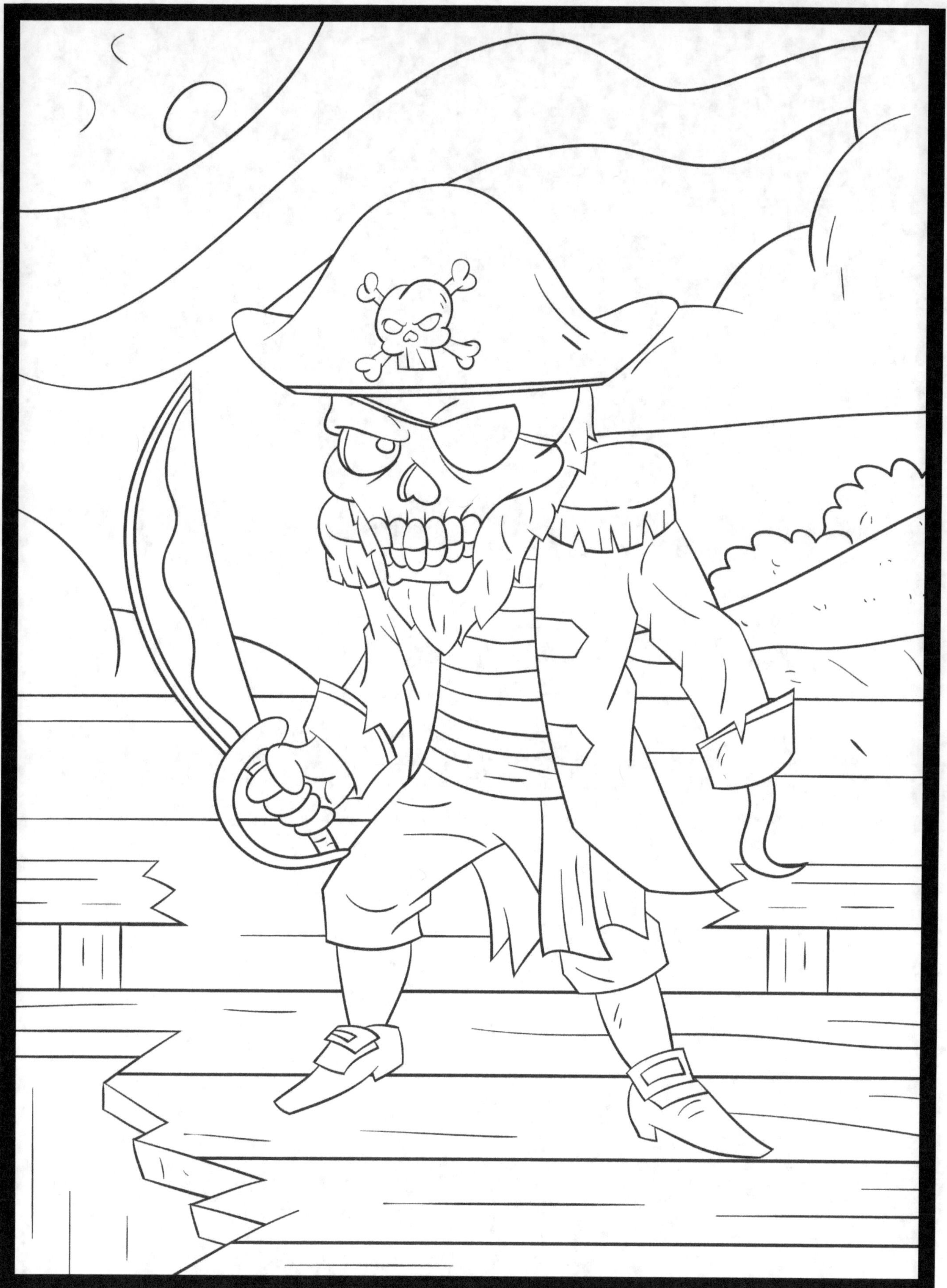

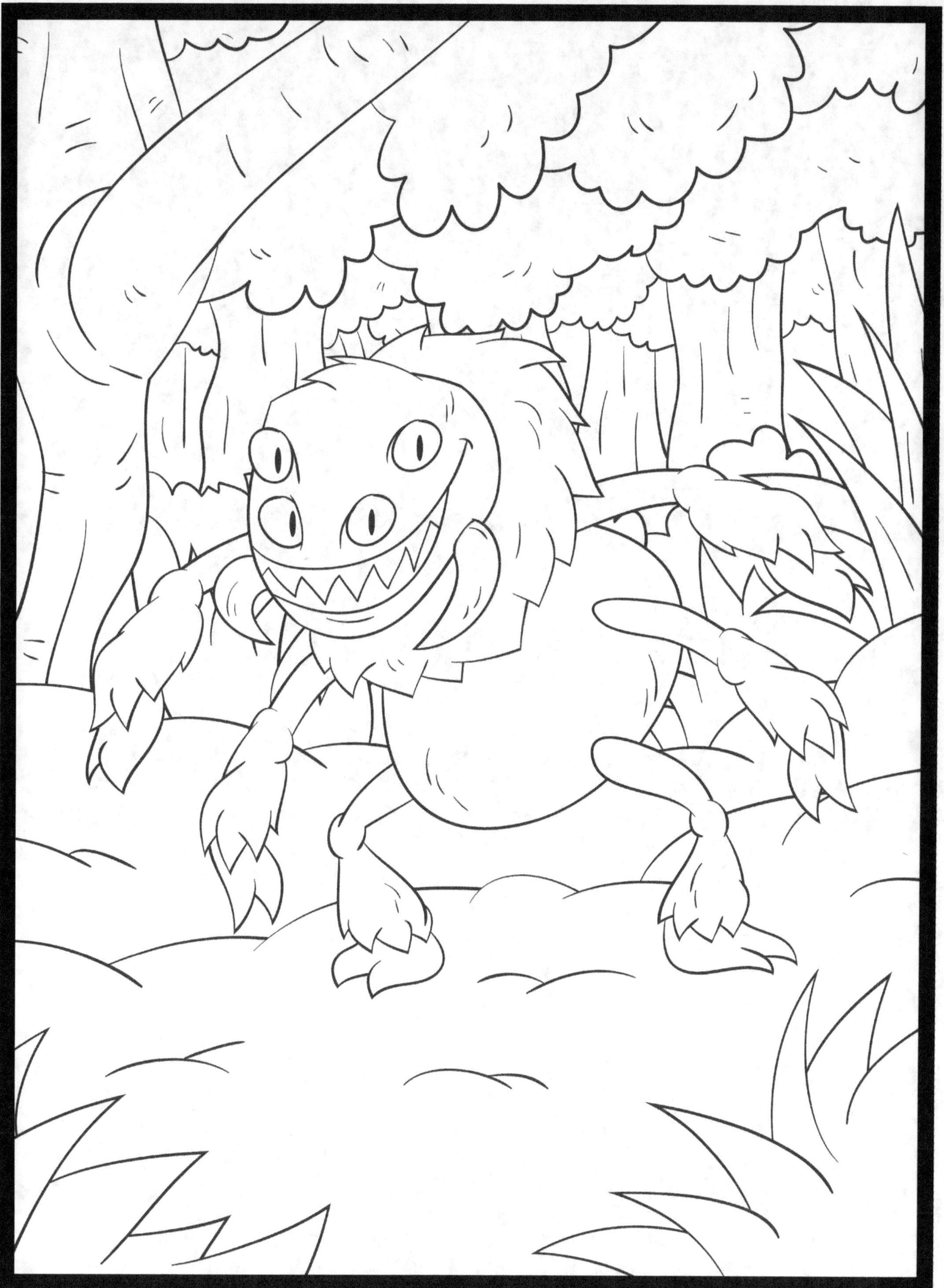

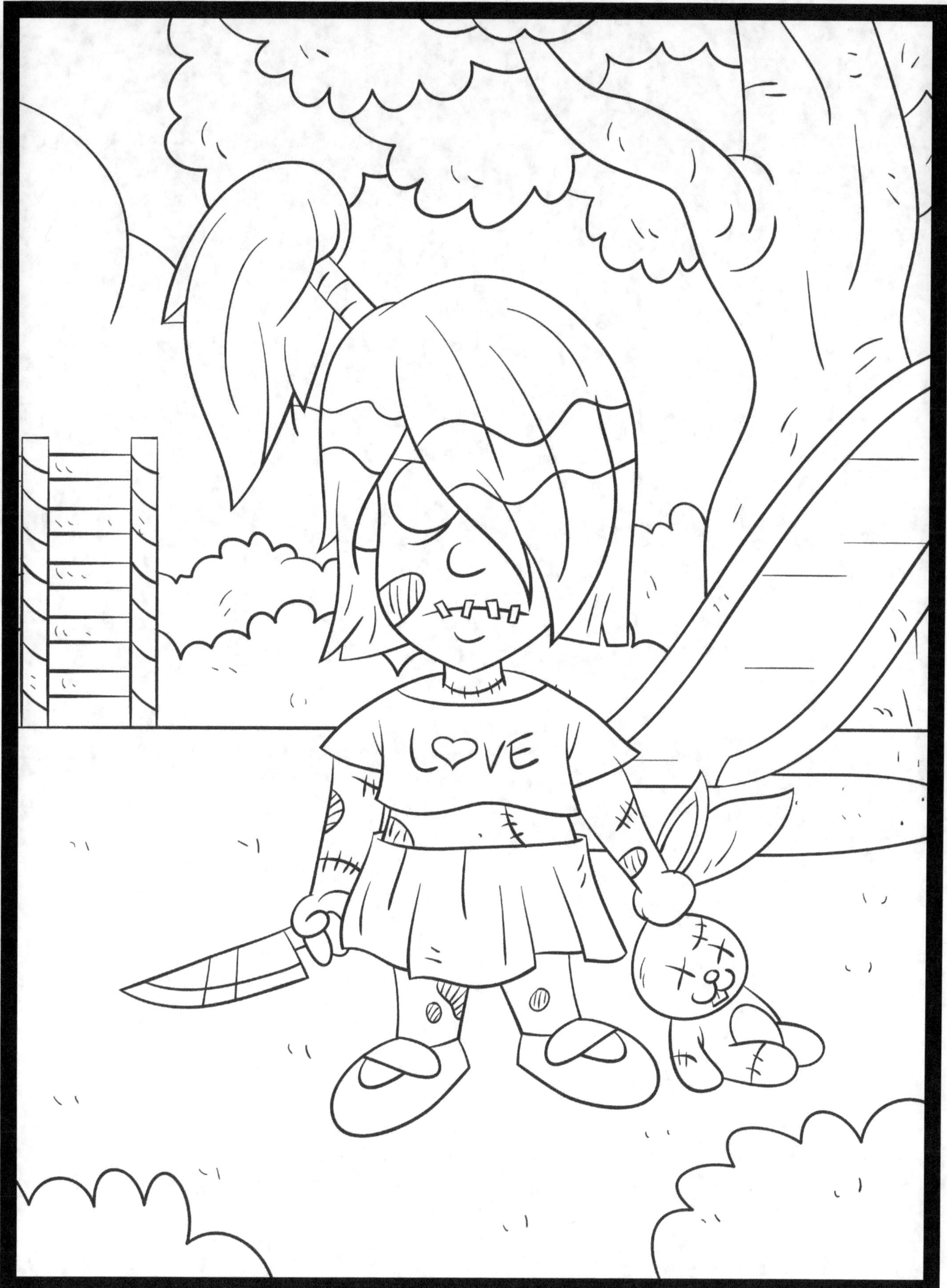

LOVE

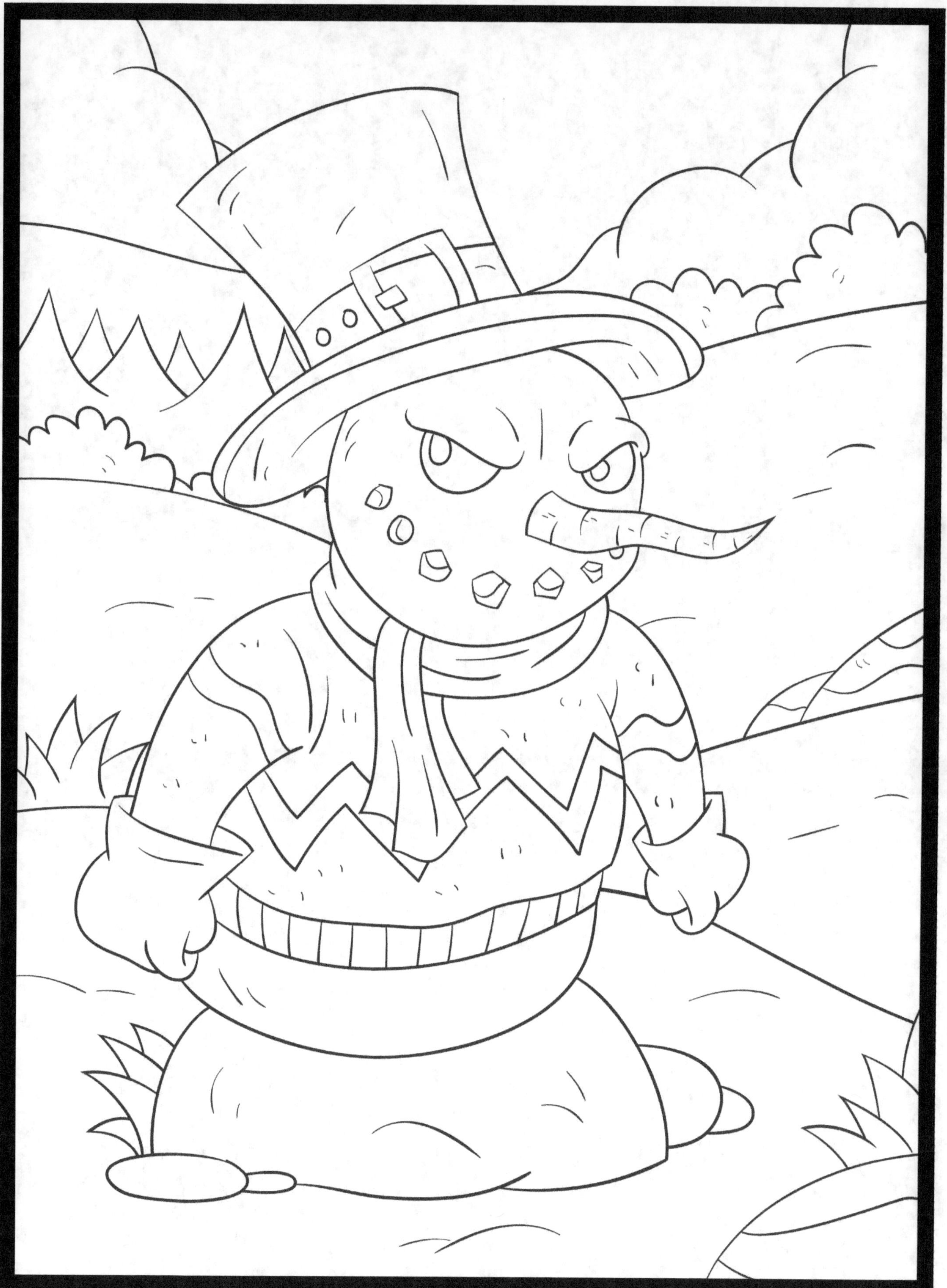

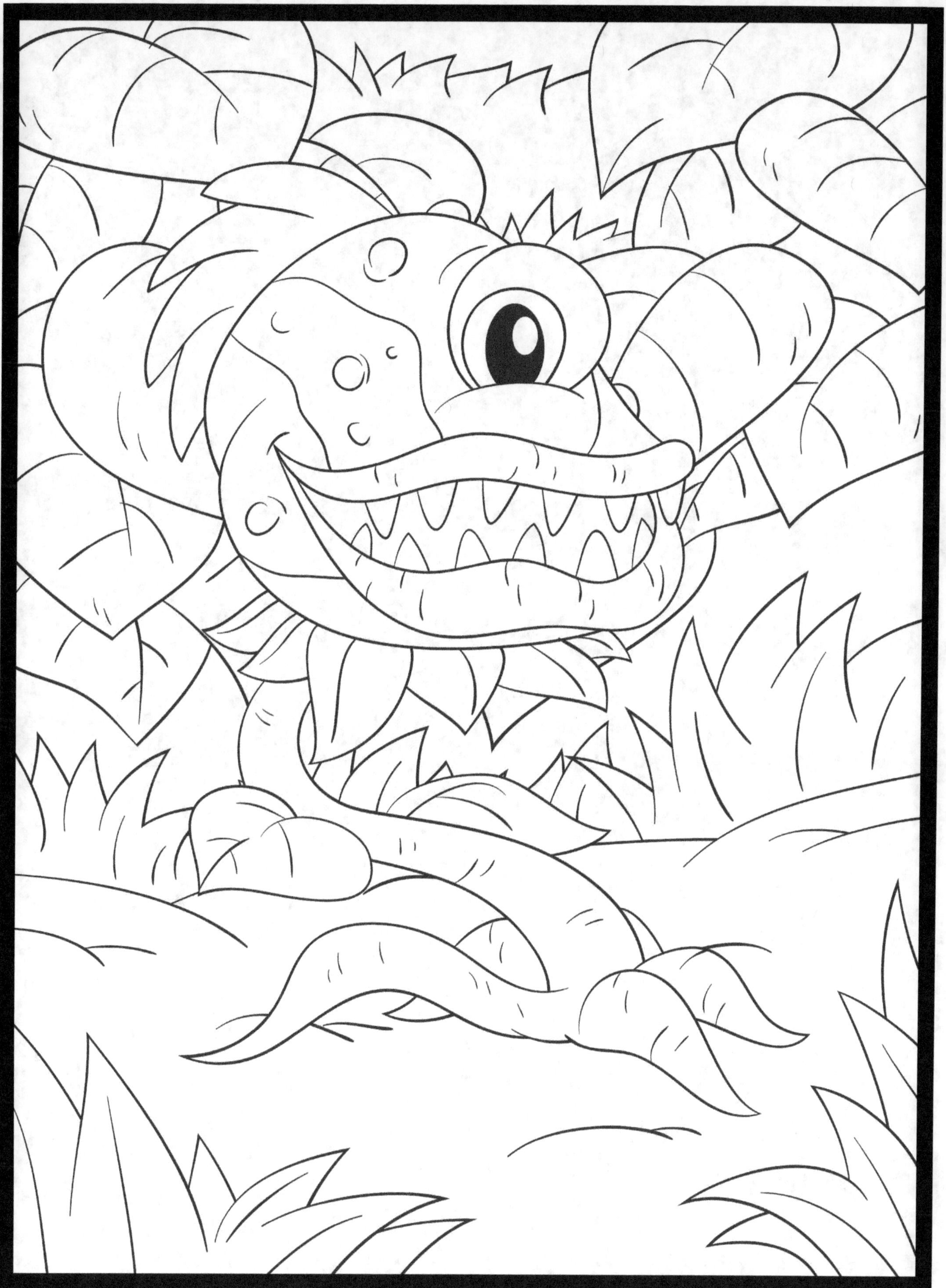

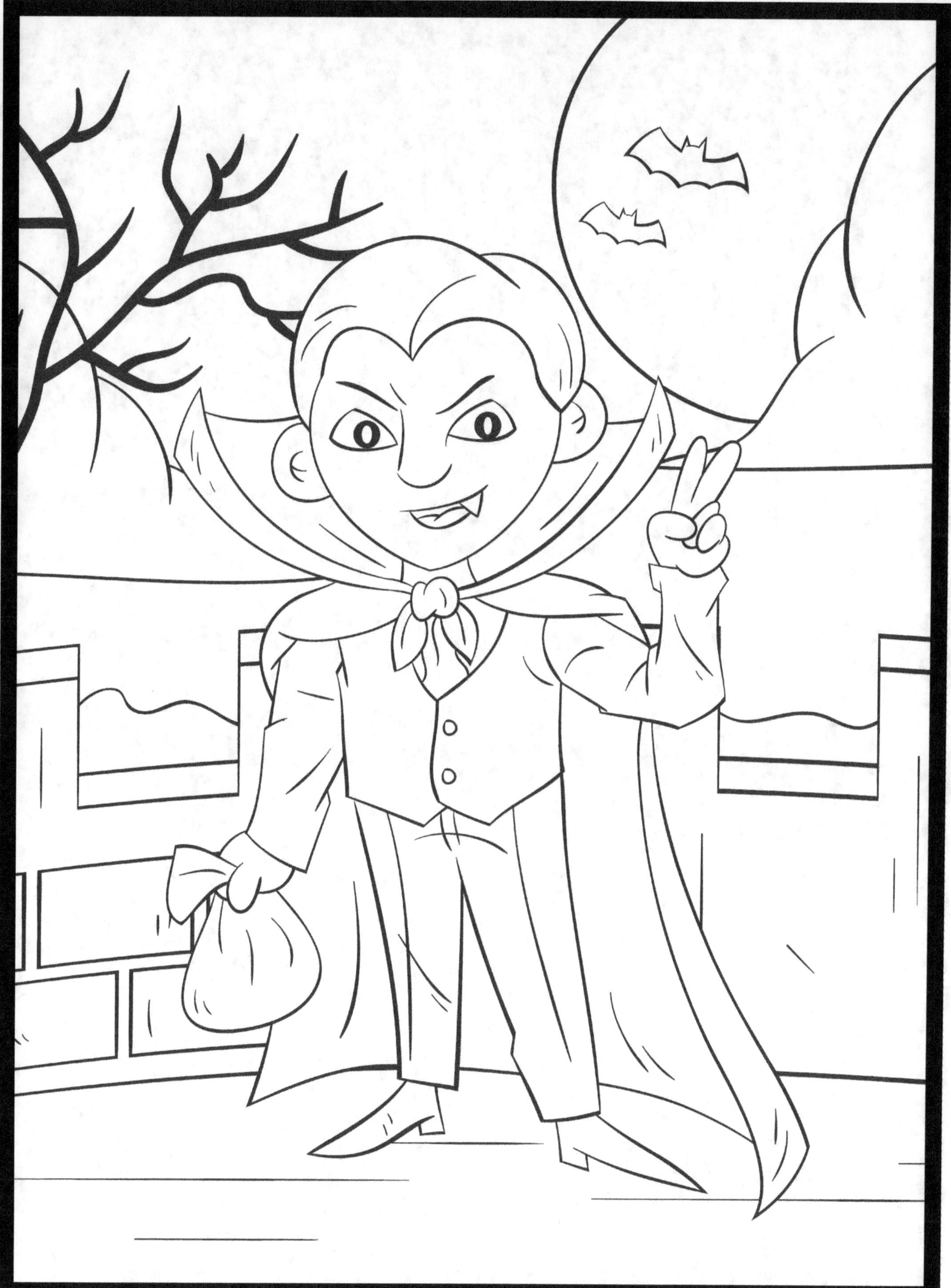

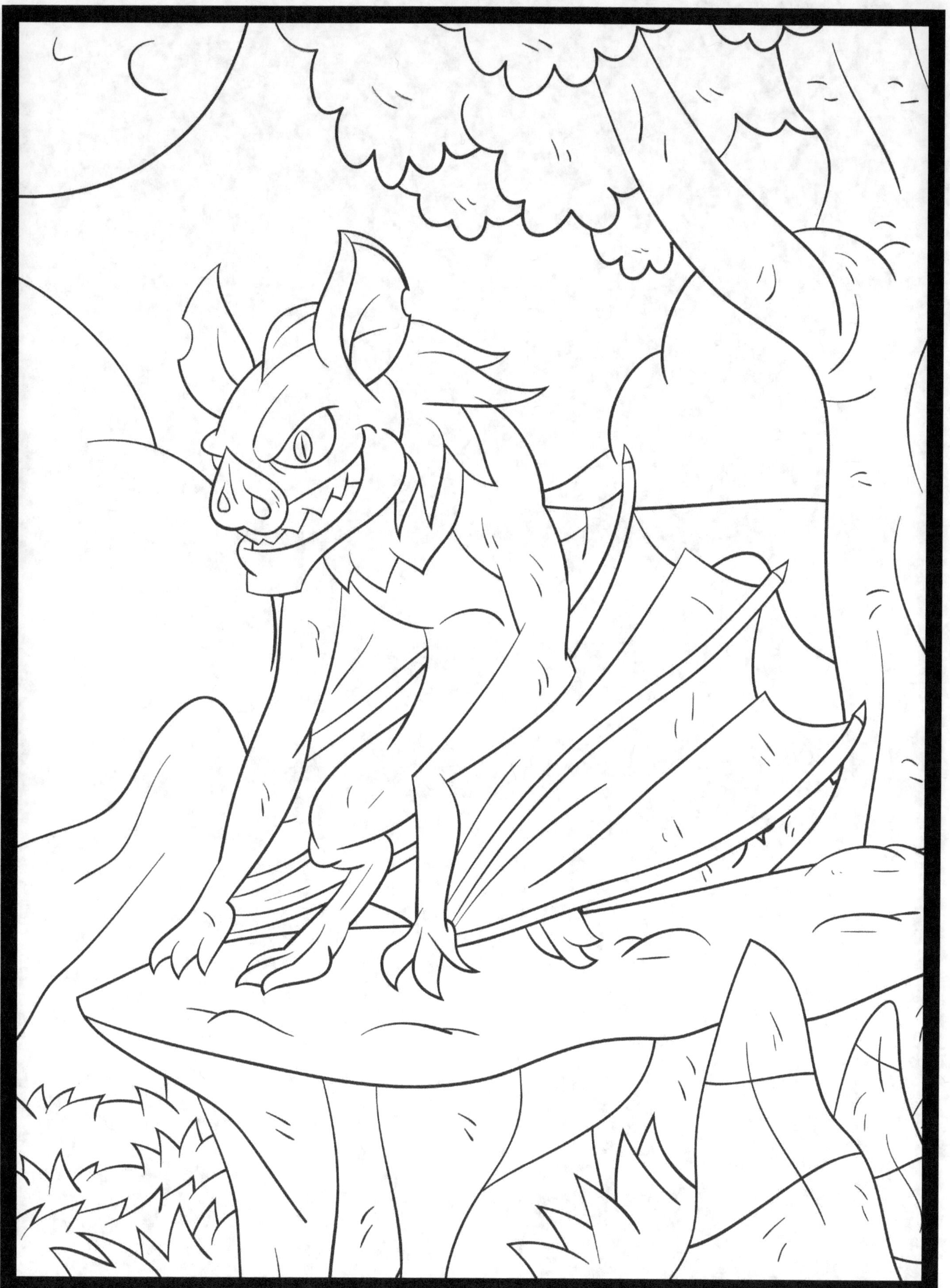